Table of Contents

Before we begin I want to warn that the following may contain sensitive content, as it aims to provide a vivid, first-person perspective on experiences with trauma, anxiety, and panic attacks.

Part One

1

The Pale White Hallway

Fluorescent hospital lights casted a sterile, almost alien glow on the stark white walls and gleaming steel surfaces. The air was thick with the sharp, acrid tang of disinfectant, the pervasive reminder that became the backdrop to my early childhood a world away from the warmth of home. Born with a cleft lip and palate, my life was not a gentle unfolding of carefree days, but a relentless cycle of hospital visits. Each surgery was a daunting ordeal, a painful intrusion into the fragile sanctuary of my young existence.

The car rides to the hospital were filled with a forced cheerfulness. My mother, ever the optimist, would try to distract me with stories and songs, but the fear was a palpable shadow hanging over us both. The hospital itself, with its labyrinthine corridors and the hushed tones of the medical staff, felt like a foreign planet where the rules of the outside world no longer applied. The operating room, with

its blinding lights and gleaming array of surgical instruments, was a terrifying spectacle. I felt small, an object on a conveyor belt. The faces of the surgeons, obscured by masks, were impersonal and intimidating, their voices a low hum that added to the sense of alienation.

Recovery was a place of limbo, a hazy transition between the oblivion of anesthesia and the harsh reality of the post-operative world. The pain, the nausea, the disorientation, it was a confusing jumble of sensations, surrounded by the moans of other patients in a symphony of suffering. It was a stark reminder of the vulnerability of the human body.

Within these confines, I met individuals who left indelible marks on my young soul. I remember a boy whose body was burnt over his entire body, a living testament to resilience. His skin, a patchwork of scars and grafts, revealed the intricate network of veins beneath. Yet, he possessed an infectious joy, a spark of life that defied his circumstances. He taught me about the unpredictable nature of fate and the quiet dignity of enduring pain.

Then there was the moment that imprinted itself into my memory with stark clarity. Trapped in a post-surgical haze, I watched as a small child screamed in pain and terror, his cries echoing through the small space. Then, a sudden silence. I saw the frantic movements of the nurses, the removal of the small body under a white sheet. Death was no longer an abstract concept, but a tangible reality, a specter that could claim anyone. After the white sheet covered the small body, the silence in the room felt different. I knew, without knowing how I knew, that being alone was the most dangerous thing in the world. A quiet terror took root in me then, a seed that would lie dormant for years.

2

The Waiting

The pale white hallway stretched before me like a desolate, unending landscape. It wasn't just a physical space; it was a psychological gauntlet, a passage through which I was forced to confront my deepest fears. The fluorescent lights overhead buzzed with an unsettling hum, casting a sickly, artificial glow that seemed to drain all color from the world. The air was thick and heavy, laden with the sharp, medicinal scent of antiseptic and disinfectant, a constant, visceral reminder of the clinical

environment. It clung to my nostrils, a metallic tang that made my stomach churn and my breath catch in my throat.

Each footstep echoed in the unnerving silence, a lonely, hollow sound that amplified my isolation. The rhythmic beeping of medical equipment, the muffled cries of other patients, the hushed, almost reverent tones of the medical staff—it was a cacophony of discomfort, a symphony of anxiety that reverberated through my body and mind. My hands were clammy, slick with a cold sweat that betrayed my inner turmoil. My heart pounded against my ribs, a frantic drumbeat that threatened to burst from my chest. My breath came in shallow, rapid gasps, as if the very air was being squeezed from my lungs.

My mother's presence, usually a source of comfort and strength, felt strangely distant, her words of reassurance muffled and distorted by the overwhelming fear that gripped me. She tried to distract me with stories, promises of treats and fun after the surgery, but her words seemed to bounce off the wall of dread that surrounded me. My mind was consumed by the impending ordeal, and the terrifying uncertainty of the outcome.

The waiting room, a space designed for temporary respite, became a chamber of heightened anxiety. The hard, plastic chairs offered no solace, and the magazines scattered on the tables were unreadable, their pages blurring before my eyes. We were a silent community, bound together by our shared vulnerability, our unspoken anxieties. The air was thick with tension, a palpable sense of shared suffering. The sound of a child's inconsolable crying, the hushed conversations of anxious parents, the relentless beeping of machines—it all contributed to the oppressive atmosphere.

Time, normally a steady, predictable flow, became distorted, elastic. Each minute stretched into an eternity, an agonizing crawl towards the inevitable. I watched the clock on the wall, its hands moving with agonizing slowness, as if mocking my impatience. I fidgeted, shifted in my seat, tried to find a comfortable position, but there was no comfort to be found in the clinical confines of the waiting room. I felt trapped, a prisoner of my own fear, with no escape from the impending ordeal.

Finally, the moment I had been dreading, the moment I had been simultaneously anticipating and fearing, arrived. My name was called, a stark, impersonal sound that echoed through the room. My heart leaped into my throat as I followed the nurse down the hallway, my footsteps echoing loudly in the unnerving silence. The closer I got to the operating room, the more intense the fear became, a suffocating wave of dread that threatened to overwhelm me. It was a physical sensation as much as an emotional one, a tightening in my chest, a knot in my stomach, a cold sweat that slicked my skin.

The operating room itself was a terrifying spectacle, a clinical space that seemed designed to maximize fear. The bright, unforgiving lights, the gleaming, menacing instruments, the masked, anonymous faces of the surgeons all of it was alien and terrifying. I felt like a small, helpless creature being led to the slaughterhouse, stripped of all agency and control.

As I was wheeled into the operating room, I made a conscious decision to shut out the world, to retreat into myself. I squeezed my eyes shut, burying my face in my hands, trying to block out the sights, the sounds, the very atmosphere of the room. I didn't want to see the instruments, didn't want to witness the preparations, didn't want to acknowledge the reality of what was about to happen. I wanted to escape, to disappear, to cease to exist.

The last thing I remember before drifting into the oblivion of anesthesia was the cold, clinical air of the operating room, the bright lights blurring into a single, blinding glare. There was no comforting touch, no reassuring presence. Only the stark reality of the moment, the knowledge that I was alone, adrift in a sea of fear. And then, the darkness descended, swallowing me whole, pulling me into the silent, unknowable void of unconsciousness. It was a surrender, a temporary escape from the terror, but it was also a step into the unknown, a leap of faith into the hands of strangers. This was more than just a medical procedure; it was a battle against my own fear, a defiance of the anxiety that threatened to consume me. It was a moment of extreme vulnerability, but also a testament to the enduring strength of the human spirit.

3

The Descent

The unforgiving chill of the operating table seeped through the thin sheet beneath me, a stark contrast to the frantic heat that clawed at my throat. Each time I was brought to this place, a silent, desperate ritual unfolded. My eyelids clamped shut, a futile attempt to barricade my mind against the looming reality. But even in the manufactured darkness behind my lashes, the terror was a tangible presence. The sharp, medicinal tang that hung heavy in the air, the brilliant, unwavering glare of the surgical lights I refused to acknowledge, the unsettling symphony of beeps and clicks from unseen machines, the masked figures gliding with an unnerving, purposeful silence, each element amplified the suffocating dread. Every shallow breath was a whispered countdown, each frantic thrum of my own heart a desperate drumbeat against the approaching void.

The beginning was always the same, a chillingly familiar routine. The smooth, cool pressure of the plastic mask molding to the contours of my face. Then, the insidious sweetness of the gas, a cloying, artificial aroma that feigned the innocent scent of watermelon, began its unwelcome invasion. It started subtly, a strange lightness blossoming in my head and across my cheeks, as if the very laws of gravity were momentarily suspended, teasing me with a fleeting sense of escape. But this lightness quickly morphed into a terrifying surrender, my own body betraying me, my limbs growing heavy and distant, like a marionette with its strings carelessly severed.

And then it would wash over me, the overwhelming, disorienting rush of sensation, a bizarre paradox of weightless prickles that skittered across my skin, a grotesque prelude to the encroaching oblivion. Sounds twisted and elongated, the steady, life-affirming pulse of the cardiac monitor dissolving into a distorted, fading hum, the hushed, clinical tones of the surgical team bleeding into an echoing nothingness. Everything receded, pulled inexorably into a vast, inky abyss. And then... the final surrender. Consciousness flickered and died, plunging me into the total, absolute blankness of a world without sensation, without thought, without being. Just... out.

The return to consciousness was never a swift ascent, but rather a gradual surfacing from a deep, dark well. Fragmented thoughts flickered like dying embers before slowly, painstakingly, igniting into awareness. Each awakening deposited me in a slightly different reality. A new room, a different arrangement of humming machines, unfamiliar shadows dancing on the walls. Yet, the constant was the gentle vigilance of the nurses, their smiles, a silent language of reassurance, and a shared understanding of the painful ordeal I had just endured. "You're with us now," their soft voices would convey, "and you were so brave."

As the fog of anesthesia began to recede, a great wave of liberation washed over me, a lightness that momentarily overshadowed the nascent throbbing that pulsed beneath my skin. The suffocating grip of pre-operative terror, the icy tendrils of dread that had coiled around my heart, had vanished, leaving behind a fragile sense of triumph.

Now, a new adversary emerged. The dull, persistent ache that resonated through my small body. But this pain felt different, somehow external, a tangible hurdle to overcome in the bright, unfiltered light of being awake. The simple act of existing, of drawing breath and seeing the world around me, held a fierce allure that diminished the discomfort.

My head, still heavy with the lingering effects of the anaesthesia, felt like a leaden weight pressing into the pillow. The room swam in dizzying circles, the fluorescent lights above blurring into hazy halos. My limbs, disconnected and unresponsive, lay like cumbersome anchors, defying any attempt at movement. Yet, from the depths of this groggy inertia, an ingrained instinct stirred. My first words, a hoarse whisper that barely disturbed the quiet, were a desperate plea for the familiar: "Can you go tell my parents I'm awake?"

Their arrival was like the breaking of dawn after a long night. Their worried yet relieved faces, brimming with love and concern, cut through the sterile anonymity of the recovery room. And despite the insistent crescendo of pain that accompanied every shallow breath, a fierce, unwavering determination solidified within me.

"I want to go home," I'd insist, my voice thin but resolute. "I'm ready."

The recovery room, with its bland walls and humming equipment, held a singular promise: escape, and that escape was paved with the brightly colored, artificially flavored currency of childhood. Jell-O and popsicles. These sugary treats, however, were not the comfort they were meant to be. My young body, still reeling from the invasion it had just experienced, viewed them with suspicion. Each wobbly spoonful of Jell-O, its synthetic sweetness clinging to my tongue, sent a nauseating wave rolling through my stomach, the room tilting precariously. Each icy lick of the popsicle, its saccharine chill a stark contrast to the inner turmoil, felt strangely abrasive, a minor penance on the path to freedom. Yet, the yearning for the familiar embrace of home, the soft comfort of my own bed, fueled a stubborn resilience that belied my small stature. I persevered. Each bite that I forced myself to swallow was a tiny act of defiance against my body's protests. Every bite was also a step closer to the coveted discharge papers and the promise of healing within the safe, familiar walls of home. And so, this peculiar ritual became an indelible part of my post-operative experience. The gentle summons of the awakening nurse, the blessed arrival of my parents, the reluctant, almost painful consumption of sugary salvation, and finally, the slow, precious journey back to the sanctuary of home, where the real healing could begin.

4

The Hammer and the Hip: A Seven-Year-Old's Nightmare

At the tender age of seven, nestled within the fleeting normalcy of 90s suburbia, a new pronouncement shattered my fragile peace.

This wasn't just another surgery; this was the most significant one yet. It was a double whammy, a complex medical feat that promised radical transformation at a staggering personal cost. The doctors planned to meticulously harvest cartilage from the back of my ear to reconstruct the delicate shape of my nostril. Even more daunting, they would take bone from my hip to build a sturdy bridge for my nose. I had no idea the world of discomfort that awaited me in the recovery room.

During the frequent, unsettling visits leading up to this monumental event, I'd find myself a silent, often bored, spectator in clinical meeting rooms. Adults in crisp white coats would dissect and discuss my face, my future, their voices, a low drone of medical jargon. The air hung heavy with the clean, sharp scent of disinfectants, a smell that would forever be etched into my memory as a prelude to dread. But there was one doctor who consistently broke the pattern, stepping out from the professional detachment of the others.

An orthodontist, he would invariably pull me aside after these general visits, speaking to me one-on-one, his words cutting through the quiet hum of the room with chilling clarity.He told me, unequivocally, that this surgery was going to be very, very painful. The recovery, he warned, would be brutal: two months of no walking and a grueling two weeks of continuous monitoring at the hospital. His stark pronouncements didn't just inform me; they solidified my worst nightmares, dragging them from the shadowy corners of my mind into the harsh, unforgiving light of reality. My heart hammered against my ribs, a frantic drumbeat against the wall of my chest, and a bone-deep terror took root. A fierce dislike, bordering on hatred, for this doctor blossomed within me. Unlike the fleeting glimmers of empathy I might have felt from others in the past, he offered none, only cold, clinical facts delivered with an unsettling lack of warmth.

The surgery was set for six agonizing months after that initial, terrifying visit. And throughout those six months, the grim countdown played out in the background of my daily life. I continued to have my regular orthodontist appointments, with this particular doctor always in attendance, his presence a constant shadow. Each time I saw him, his very being was a chilling reminder, and he would invariably reiterate the impending pain, detailing the suffering that awaited me with a relentless insistence. Just seeing him, his face a grim harbinger of the future, would trigger a wave of overwhelming anxiety and panic. Prior to him, the orthodontist's office had been merely a tedious chore, never a source of fear. Now, with him around, it became a constant, unwelcome prelude to the hell I would soon endure, a recurring nightmare made flesh.

The day before the surgery, the finality of it all pressed down on me. I had one last orthodontist appointment to remove anything in my mouth, my braces, my wires, any hardware that might impede the upcoming procedures. And there he was again, this unyielding prophet of pain. He looked at me, a terrified seven-year-old on the precipice of unimaginable suffering, and delivered his final, cruel reminder. He told me, his voice devoid of any softening, that I would be in such agonizing pain that I wouldn't be able to walk for two weeks. Then, he added, with chilling, unforgettable specificity, that "it's going to feel like someone taking a hammer and smashing it over your hips."

I left that appointment sobbing uncontrollably, my small body racked with tremors, my soul pouring out in raw, guttural tears to my mom and dad. I was beyond scared, beyond nervous, beyond something that would take me decades to understand. .. Every fiber of my being screamed in protest. I had already navigated my own personal hell countless times, had woken up in strange rooms, endured procedures I couldn't comprehend, and battled back to a semblance of normalcy again and again. Of course, that night before the surgery, sleep was an impossible refuge. Every word he had uttered, every horrifying possibility of pain and suffering, hammered in my mind, echoing the very sensation he had so graphically described. I lay awake, suspended in raw terror, watching the hours crawl by, waiting for the inevitable dawn that would lead me back into the nightmare. There was no escape, only the slow march towards what felt like an inevitable, devastating impact.

5

The Impossible Walk

The world after the surgery was a hazy, disorienting blur. My body felt heavy, alien, as if it belonged to someone else. The pain, a dull, throbbing ache, pulsed through my newly reconstructed nose, face, ears, hips, a constant reminder of the ordeal I had just endured. But amidst the discomfort, a fierce determination began to simmer within me. I was done with being confined to a bed, done with the sterile, antiseptic smell of the hospital. I wanted to walk. More than that, I needed to walk.

The nurses, with their gentle but firm voices, urged me to rest, to take the pain medication, to allow my body to heal. But their words were like whispers in a hurricane, drowned out by the roar of my own stubborn will. I was eight years old, and I had already endured more than most adults. I was not going to be held back.

I needed to use the washroom, but I didn't want help. I wanted to do it myself. Something sparked in me to just get up and do it, as if the pain didn't exist. The first attempt was a staggering, almost comical failure, driven by the sudden, urgent need to go. My legs, weak and unsteady, buckled beneath me, and I collapsed back onto the bed, a wave of frustration washing over me, mixed with the uncomfortable urgency. But even as I lay there, gasping for breath, the determination only grew stronger. I would not be defeated, and I would not be denied the simple dignity of using the restroom.

The second attempt was slightly better. I managed to stand, my body trembling, my head spinning. The room swayed around me, the walls tilting at an alarming angle.

But I refused to give in. I took a tentative step, then another, my feet shuffling across the cold linoleum floor. Each step was a victory, a defiant act against the pain and weakness that threatened to consume me.

The bathroom, a mere few feet away, seemed like an impossible distance. But I was determined to reach it, to prove to myself that I was still in control of my body. The journey was agonizing, each step a battle against the pain that radiated from my nose, the dizziness that threatened to send me crashing to the floor. My mom, her face a mixture of concern and encouragement, walked beside me, her strong hand gently supporting my arm. I felt a surge of gratitude for her unwavering support, for her belief in me. She was my rock, my anchor, and her presence gave me the strength to persevere.

The return journey, back to the bed, was even more challenging. My body was exhausted, my resolve wavering. But I had made it once, and I could make it again. I leaned heavily against the wall, using it as a crutch, my hand trailing along the cold, smooth surface.

Each step was a testament to my willpower, a defiant roar against the pain and weakness that threatened to consume me.

I was so excited, so filled with a triumphant energy, that I turned to my mom and said, "Let's go home." I did the impossible. I wanted to go heal at home instead of sitting here in this hospital bed. I had somehow managed to walk, even though it was meant to be medically impossible. I was beyond proud of myself and I wanted to celebrate that victory by going home.

My mom called the nurses and told them what I had just done. They were astonished, and you could see the happiness in their eyes. Unfortunately, a doctor had to clear me, and at two in the morning, none were on the floor. If I could do it again in the morning when they were here, I was sure they would sign me off and let me go home.

My mom and I looked at each other. I accepted it. This was a battle I would have to fight all over again, even if it was going to hurt even more. I couldn't sleep. I was in too much pain but refused to use the painkillers. I was too eager to prove to the doctors that I had just done the impossible. So I just lay there, waiting for time to pass.

I watched the sunrise. My mom woke up and stepped out of the room to call my dad, telling him we were awake and he could come visit. I waited patiently, with the excitement of a kid on Christmas morning. My dad entered the room smiling, his arms full of presents and cards from my schoolmates. After opening everything, I felt a new drive surge through me. I was ready to get up and do it again.

"Let's go get the doctor," I said. "Let's tell him what I can do, and let's get the hell out of here."

The doctor arrived a few hours later. I told him what I had done the night before. With a look of pure disbelief on his face, he said, "No way you did that. That's medically impossible."

He paused, then pointed to the meal tray.

"Tell you what. You eat this Jell-O, this freezie, and some of this food, and you can go."

As much as I hated the idea, I devoured everything in front of him before he could even leave the room. He looked at me and laughed. "Tough guy, eh? Okay. Tell you what. You walk down the hall to the elevator, and I'll let you leave."

My eyes, my head, my heart—everything went spinning. The elevator seemed miles away. This was something I knew I couldn't do. *Can't?* The word echoed in my mind. I don't think so. It was time to shake off the fear of the pain and prove to everyone I could do it. "Let's do this thing," I said, my voice steadier than I felt.

The impossible walk to the elevator was a similar struggle, but on a larger scale. The hallway stretched before me like an endless desert, the elevator a distant oasis. My father, his face with a mixture of concern and pride, was beside me, standing at the threshold of my recovery room doorway. His presence was a silent encouragement.

It was time to shake off the fear of the pain and prove to everyone I could do it. "Let's do this thing," I said, my voice steadier than I felt.

The elevator felt like a marathon, though in reality, it was maybe a hundred feet. But seeing that distance, that finish line, only made me want to conquer it more. Halfway there, I was exhausted. Excruciating pain shot through me with every shuffle. My body screamed at me to give up. That's when my dad's voice cut through the haze.

"Halfway there, guy!" he said, his voice firm, "you can't give up now. It's either your own bed in a few hours, or it's back to that room over there. Your choice."

His words were the fuel I needed. I pushed the thought of giving up out of my head, fought back against the pain, and just kept walking. The walk was slow, agonizing, each step a victory against the pain and weakness that threatened to consume me. But I refused to give in. I was eight years old, and I had already learned that the human spirit was capable of extraordinary feats. I had learned that determination could overcome any obstacle, that the impossible was merely a challenge waiting to be conquered. I didn't stop until my hand slapped the cool metal of the elevator button.

My dad called over to the nurses, who I now saw were watching, silently cheering me on. They gave the doctor a nod. I did it. I leaned against the wall, breathing heavily, and made my declaration to anyone listening. "I made it to the elevator. I'm not going back to that room. I'm going home. And that's final."

My mom quickly grabbed our things from the room, and the three of us stood together. We rode down that elevator together. The elevator of victory. As the doors opened and closed with other people coming in and out, I could feel it all wash over me. I knew in that moment that I had accomplished something truly remarkable. This walk, this seemingly insignificant act, became a symbol of my resilience, a testament to my unwavering spirit. It was a moment of triumph, a victory against the pain and weakness that had plagued my young life. It was a moment that would shape my understanding of myself, a moment that would teach me that I was stronger than I ever imagined, and that with the support of those who loved me, I could overcome any challenge.

6

The Pursuit of Normalcy

The world outside the hospital room, the familiar suburban landscape of the 90s, always felt like a distant, vibrant dream when I was confined to recovery.

In an era before the instant gratification of the internet, before cell phones tethered us to endless information and communication, convalescence was a slow, deliberate act. My childhood was punctuated by these intense, isolating periods of recuperation, each one a grueling, solitary battle against physical pain, yet always fueled by a single, powerful mantra echoing in my young mind: "Get back to normal so I can see my friends again."

My days at home, confined by the demands of healing, became a relentless exercise in defiance. I would force my small body to push through the lingering aches, the dull throbs that resonated within my bones, and the tender soreness of fresh incisions. Every ounce of effort was aimed at a singular, overriding goal: to be outside, to feel the sun on my face, to hear the laughter of my friends. The intention was simple yet imperative – to play, to be a goofball, to unleash the boundless energy of childhood. I longed for my stomach to ache from laughter, instead of surgery. And in those precious moments of unbridled joy, surrounded by the echoes of childish glee, the pain – both physical and emotional – would miraculously recede, fading into the background like a forgotten bad dream. It was a perfect escape, a temporary, desperately needed reprieve from the harsh, undeniable reality of what my body endured.

My cousin, now best friend and I were inseparable, a dynamic duo against the boundless boredom of suburban summer days. Our lives were a blur of reckless bike rides down gravel paths, scraped knees earned from constructing precarious forts deep in the woods, the exhilarating thrill of hurtling down hills in makeshift pushcarts, and the sheer audacity of running wild through the local mall like a pair of giddy, uninhibited idiots, sometimes avoiding security guards.These were the moments I craved with an almost visceral hunger, the immersive, carefree chaos that pulled me away from the lingering memory of bright, clinical rooms and aching, vulnerable wounds.

Crucially, throughout all of this, I never wanted to be seen as a charity case. Pity was a foreign concept I actively rejected, an uncomfortable emotion I recoiled from. I yearned to be normal, to be treated like any other kid on the block, without special allowances or hushed tones.

My older brother, just a year and a half my senior, became my steadfast protector, not by coddling me or treating me with kid gloves, but by treating me exactly as an older brother should. We fought, we wrestled on the living room floor until furniture shook, we played street hockey until dusk obscured the net, and yes, he often got the better of me in our impromptu brawls, leaving me with playful bruises. But this was precisely what I wanted from him. I knew, in some unspoken way, that he was a silent witness to my childhood suffering, yet our relationship was forged in the crucible of typical sibling rivalry, a powerful testament to the normalcy I desperately craved. If anyone dared to mock or tease me – a mercifully rare occurrence, though it did happen – he would transform into a fierce guardian, standing up for me until the bitter end, a silent, unwavering loyalty that spoke volumes about our bond.

My greatest fear during those arduous recoveries wasn't the discomfort itself, or even the potential for future surgeries. It was the sympathetic glances from adults, the hushed, concerned tones when they spoke about me, the subtle shifts in their expressions. Those were the moments that truly unsettled me, signaling that my condition was serious, that I wasn't "normal." I detested those times with every fiber of my being. I wanted to play. I wanted to go back to school. More than anything, I needed to go back to school.

Returning to the chaotic, vibrant energy of the classroom was like stepping back into my rightful place in the world. My friends, with the easy, unburdened acceptance of childhood, welcomed me back as if I'd never been gone, their enthusiasm genuine and immediate. Of course, nobody knew the full extent of the hell I'd navigated, the immense pain and sheer resilience it had taken to simply return to their midst. And I never spoke of it. The real reason for my silence was a deeply ingrained separation; that part of my life, those traumatic hospital stays, existed in a different, walled-off compartment of my being. I believed, perhaps correctly, that no one would truly understand if I tried to articulate the raw, isolating depths of it. How could they? Their childhoods weren't punctuated by surgical scars and the smell of watermelon-flavored gas or needles.

Besides, I had finally escaped my personal hell, and my sole ambition, my driving force, was to smile again. The quickest, most effective path to my own elusive happiness, I discovered, was by actively making other people happy. I became the unofficial purveyor of stupid jokes, the energetic catalyst for classroom laughter, a human sponge absorbing every ounce of positive energy in the room. I craved to be surrounded by smiling, joyful faces, convinced that if I immersed myself thoroughly enough in their happiness, I would eventually feel it, even if the inside of me still felt like complete shit. It was a conscious, desperate strategy to combat the lingering shadows.

7

The Relentless Cycle: The Whisper, The Panic, The Drive to Hell

Life in suburbia, specifically the vibrant, sun-drenched, pre-digital suburbia of the 1990s, was a meticulously crafted facade for me. It was a tableau of scraped knees on asphalt, broken bones,the distant 'thwack!' of a hockey stick and ball, and the comforting static of late-night cartoons, usually The Simpsons on a bulky television. This was the "normal" I fought so desperately to reclaim after each surgical ordeal. I plunged back into it with a fierce, almost desperate hunger, craving the mundane, the predictable, the comforting noise of life unfettered by scalpels and recovery rooms. It was an elaborate, exhausting illusion, sustained by sheer force of will and the boundless, often reckless energy of childhood.

My early years were a constant flux and flow between the ordinary joys of being a kid and the stark, demanding reality of my medical needs. Weeks would blur into what felt like a truly endless series of appointments. As my young brain rapidly developed, absorbing the world like a sponge, so too did the intricacies of my medical care. There were countless hours spent in speech therapy, often in a small, quiet room with a patient therapist, working on exercises to ensure I'd be able to articulate words properly as my facial structure changed. Then came the hundreds of orthodontist appointments, the relentless pressure of braces and expanders, meticulously straightening teeth that were constantly shifting in response to the growth and changes in my jaw and face.

The strange blessing and undeniable curse of my vivid, almost photographic memory meant I absorbed every detail of these sessions. I'd spend what felt like eons in impersonal meeting rooms, surrounded by a rotating cast of doctors – my oral surgeon, the orthodontist, specialists whose titles I barely grasped – all leaning over charts, discussing my face, my progress, and the next steps, all in a language utterly alien to a developing mind. School days were constantly interrupted, punctuated by these crucial appointments, each absence a minor disruption to my carefully cultivated "normal." Yet, surprisingly, anxiety wasn't the dominant emotion at this stage. I perfected the art of mental disconnection, not out of fear of the medical jargon, but out of sheer, unadulterated boredom. What stimulating engagement could a five-to-seven-year-old find amidst adults droning on about things they couldn't possibly grasp, surrounded by a handful of sticky, well-used push-and-pull toys and faded picture books that had seen too many clumsy hands? No thanks!

When these medical excursions finally concluded, a profound sense of relief would wash over me. My mom and I would return home, and I'd shed the clinical atmosphere like an old skin, rushing back to my best friend's house, diving headfirst into our games as if the past ten hours had simply ceased to exist. I was back to being a goofball, back to making stupid jokes that only we found hilarious, back to the carefree, authentic me.

Once I was settled back into the comforting, predictable routine of school, the entire medical part of my life would recede entirely, ignored and dismissed. It was as if each surgery I endured, each painful procedure, was miraculously destined to be my very last. Just trying to live past the pain until it receded, never to be spoken of.

I lived in that optimistic, self-deluding bubble, wholeheartedly convinced that the worst was behind me. That chilling, inevitable phone call would always happen. It was never a casual mention. My mom would pull me aside, often in the quiet intimacy of our home, usually after dinner when the day's distractions were winding down, or sometimes, more jarringly, as I was settling into bed, my mind already drifting towards dreams of adventures. Her voice would take on a softer, more deliberate, almost apologetic tone. "Matt," she'd begin, her words carefully chosen, delivered with a gentle solemnity that would immediately send a shiver down my spine. "We have a surgery in the morning. I wanted to let you know so you won't be surprised."

And with those words, a tidal wave hit. Anxiety, a monstrous, unwelcome guest I had briefly managed to banish, slammed back into my brain with immediate, brutal force. There was no gentle re-entry; it welcomed itself back with a vengeance. The carefully constructed walls around that part of my life crumbled in an instant. I would cry, genuine, heartbroken pleas spilling from my lips, my small body seized by a visceral panic. I'd beg and bargain with my parents, until sheer exhaustion, both physical and emotional, finally forced me to accept my fate and surrender to the absolute hell I knew I was about to be sucked right back into.

See, the thing is, as I got older and my brain was developing more, as I moved from a little kid to a school-aged child and then a pre-teen, I started to understand more. My active, increasingly capable brain would relentlessly conjure the worst-case scenarios, playing them out in vivid, terrifying detail, each image more horrifying than the last. The innocent disconnection of a young mind was replaced by the agonizing dread of a conscious mind.

Sleep, on those nights, was an impossible dream, a cruel mirage. The hours crawled by, each tick of the clock amplifying the knot of dread in my stomach. And when it was finally time to leave the house, the journey to the hospital began. I don't know if anyone can truly visualize this, this profound, chilling shift. But imagine, for a moment, driving down the same familiar street every single day, a route synonymous with comfort, with home, with safety. Now, picture driving down that very same street, but this time, every tree, every mailbox, every familiar crack in the pavement feels fundamentally, terrifyingly different. It felt like I was losing a piece of myself with every meter traveled, shedding my identity as a normal kid. It was a waking nightmare, a grim procession driving away from my heaven, my sanctuary of normalcy, straight into hell. A dark, oppressive place that settled into the very core of my being, digging deeper with every kilometer closer to the imposing, unavoidable brick structure of the hospital. The air in the car would feel heavy, thick with unspoken fear, even as my parents tried to maintain a facade of calm.

My dad, a police officer whose precinct was conveniently close to the hospital, usually dropped my mom and me off at the front doors. The moment my feet touched the hospital's polished, institutional floors, an immediate and bone-chilling transformation occurred. That happy, smiling, joking kid, the one who lived for bike rides and stupid puns, simply vanished. In his place, a strong, silent fighter stepped forward, a stoic acceptance hardening my gaze. My chin would lift, my shoulders square. We would check in, the initial surge of anxiety usually manageable at this specific point, a low hum beneath my warrior's resolve. But as we moved through the different, familiar stages of the pre-operative routine – the waiting room, the triage nurse, the changing into the flimsy gown, the questions about allergies – the anxiety would begin its relentless, agonizing ascent. With each step, each familiar face, each scent, the panic escalated, becoming demonstrably stronger, more crushing, at every successive stage. It was a mental and emotional gauntlet.

By the time we reached the cold, brightly lit space of the pre-operative room, as I matured from a small child into a young boy and then a pre-teen, my anxiety would reach a fever pitch, overwhelming my ability to maintain any semblance of control. My physical symptoms, a horrifying betrayal of my inner strength, would take over, raw and undeniable. I would projectile vomit out of sheer, visceral fear, the violent expulsion a testament to the terror that gripped me. I would fight, lash out with desperate, flailing limbs against the nurses, cry hysterically, my voice raw and broken, until my small body, utterly depleted, finally gave up the struggle, collapsing into a silent, trembling heap.

And then, the inevitable, dreaded moment. My name would be called, resonating through the hushed room like a death knell. Fear. The overwhelming, all-consuming fear of the unknown that lay beyond those swinging doors, layered upon the crushing, horrifying fear of what I did know, what I had endured countless times before. This terrifying cycle, this relentless assault on my very soul, became the brutal, unpredictable rhythm of my childhood for fourteen agonizing years. I never knew when the last surgery would be. There was no "completion date" that my doctors or parents could offer, no definitive end in sight, no matter how many times I would ask, how desperately I would plead for an answer. The chronic uncertainty, the constant threat of another interruption, was its own special kind of torment, a shadow that never truly lifted.

Part Two

8

The Echoes of Normalcy: When the Rollercoaster Slowed, But Didn't Stop

The concept of a "final" surgery was never a definitive pronouncement in my childhood.

Instead, it was a gradual, almost imperceptible shift, a slow deceleration of the relentless medical rollercoaster that had dominated my early years. As the calendar pages turned and the years accumulated, the frantic pace of two or more surgeries a year began to mercifully slow, stretching out to perhaps one every two years. It was less a finish line marked with triumph, and more a dwindling, hopeful silence that settled between operations, allowing for longer stretches of what felt like actual childhood.

My last surgery, a deeply scarred landmark in my medical journey, took place on October 11th, 2001. I was 15 years old, teetering on the cusp of adolescence. Although no one ever officially declared it the end, a profound intuition settled within me. This felt like the grand finale, the final curtain call on a hellish performance that had dictated so much of my young life. There were no cheers, no celebratory pronouncements of "hooray," "hurrah," or "congratulations." The immense relief was a silent, internal sigh. The experience was simply muffled into the vast collection of past memories, filed away in the recesses of my mind, and life, with its indifferent, unstoppable momentum, continued on. The physical scars would fade, but the invisible ones were just beginning to surface.

In this newfound, fragile peace, a different kind of storm began to brew. It was subtle at first, an unsettling ripple beneath the surface of my hard-won normalcy. I started to experience intense anxiety, a sensation that was utterly foreign and terrifying. It wasn't the panic of an impending surgery; this was an unknown fear for me, an unsettling, bewildering understanding that I didn't yet possess the words or the life experience to comprehend. It was a phantom menace, emerging without the clear trigger of a hospital visit.

These unsettling feelings would manifest as a terrifying physical loss of control, beginning in my head. My thoughts would spin, rapidly escalating from a vague unease into a paralyzing fear of dying, a certainty that my last moments were at hand. My heart would pound like a trapped bird desperately trying to escape its cage, its frantic rhythm echoing in my ears. My breathing would become erratic – either too fast, hyperventilating until I felt lightheaded, or feeling desperately shallow, as if I couldn't pull enough air into my lungs. A dizzying sensation of spinning out of control would wash over me, quickly followed by terrifying physical symptoms: the alarming loss of feeling, a strange tingling and numbness, in my hands and toes, as if my body was shutting down piece by piece.

Then, panic would set in, a suffocating, blinding wave that drowned out all rational thought. My entire body would tremble uncontrollably, a violent, frenzied shaking that made me feel utterly powerless. My motor skills would abandon me, my legs feeling like rubber, making it impossible to walk steadily or even stand. Desperate for any semblance of relief, for an explanation, for any comfort, I would cry for help, trying frantically to explain the unexplainable, to articulate the nameless terror seizing my body and mind. My parents had divorced by this time, and I was living with my mother. I would instinctively run to her pleading, "Mom, something's wrong! Something bad is happening!"

Naturally, propelled by my obvious distress and their own concern, we went to doctors, seeking answers for these bewildering "episodes." They ran all sorts of tests – blood work, EKGs, endless examinations – diligently canceling out most heart issues and other dire physical ailments. One doctor, grasping for an explanation in the absence of a clear diagnosis, came up with the assumption that I had asthma.

He prescribed me puffers for my breathing, which, ironically, only seemed to make things worse. The very act of taking the puffer, of focusing on my breath, often intensified the very symptoms they were meant to alleviate, pushing me further into the panic. We were utterly adrift, with no clear understanding of what these episodes were, or why they were happening to me, seemingly out of nowhere, disrupting my attempts at a normal teenage life.

These terrifying occurrences continued quite frequently, a relentless, unpredictable assault on my peace, from the age of 15 until I was 17. The sudden, unbidden nature of their onset was almost as distressing as the episodes themselves. They could strike anywhere, anytime: in the middle of a class, during a casual conversation with friends, or while trying to fall asleep.

Finally, after nearly two years of this bewildering torment, a breakthrough arrived when I returned to my trusted family doctor. He, after patiently listening to my frantic descriptions and observing my lingering unease, came to the crucial conclusion: I was suffering from panic attacks. He prescribed me Ativan, a small pill with the clear instruction that if I were to ever feel a panic attack beginning, I should take it to calm the storm.

Here's the kicker, the ingrained irony that defined my immediate response: I was too scared to take the medication. The very idea of purposefully putting drugs into my system, even for the promise of relief, brought with it an almost visceral revulsion. It stirred up the unwelcome, suffocating memories of being under the influence of countless medications from my younger years – I had been pumped full of literally all of them. I vividly recalled the disorienting rush of ketamine, the heavy, dreamlike haze of morphine, the chilling descent into unconsciousness brought on by anesthesia (often accompanied by the sweet, sickly scent of nitrous oxide), and the groggy, disconnected feeling from diphenhydramine. The thought of willingly re-entering that altered state, even for a therapeutic purpose, did not sound appetizing. It felt like another surrender, another loss of control to chemicals, a chilling echo of the operating room table where my body had so often been manipulated against my will. The cure, in my mind, felt too close to the cause of my deepest anxieties.

9

The Roar of "No": Reclamation, Recurrence, and the Allure of Escape

Turning eighteen felt less like a birthday and more like a profound awakening, a seismic shift in the very ground beneath my feet. Three years had passed since my last surgery, a seemingly long stretch of time that had allowed the most glaring physical scars to fade into faint lines, almost imperceptible to the casual observer. But the internal landscape, though hidden, remained complex, a deeply etched topography of past trauma. Yet, on that particular day, a remarkable shift occurred. An almost electric surge of power coursed through me, a newfound dominion over my own existence, embodied by a single, resonant, defiant word: **"NO."**

Nobody else heard it, of course. To the outside world, it was just another day. But on my eighteenth birthday, standing alone, I unleashed it. I shouted it at the top of my lungs. Louder and louder I screamed it, a primal, guttural roar of defiance that vibrated through every cell of my being. It was more than a sound; it was an expulsion, a violent, necessary liberation of years of suppressed emotion. To finally feel that power, the sheer, unadulterated impact of that word, was exhilarating beyond measure.

Because, as of that date, I was finally, irrevocably, in control of my own life. I possessed the undeniable ability to choose, to refuse, to do what I felt was necessary for *me*, without external permission or explanation.

I remember the exact moment *"NO!"* broke free, unleashing a torrent of tears, all the pent-up pain, the corrosive fear, the deep-seated frustration of a childhood defined by medical interventions and a constant struggle for normalcy. But astonishingly, as the tears streamed down my face, washing away years of buried anguish, they quickly morphed into pure, unadulterated joy.

I looked in the mirror, truly seeing myself, perhaps for the very first time with such clarity. I saw my past reflected there – the trauma, the enduring pain, the endless cycle of fear and recovery. And in that reflection, amidst the echoes of a difficult history, all I could do was smile. It was a smile born of triumph, of hard-won self-acceptance, a testament to surviving not just the physical battles, but the psychological warfare. No matter what external chaos or uncertainty swirled around me, no matter what challenges lay ahead, my soul and my body felt definitively connected, finally speaking the same language. I was whole, not despite my past, but because of it.

This newfound wholeness empowered me to finally stand up for myself without any fear of judgment from anyone. It was a revelation. I gained huge amounts of confidence in myself, a strength I hadn't even realized was lacking, a crucial missing piece that now clicked into place with satisfying precision. I felt on top of the world, invincible even, brimming with an energy I hadn't known I possessed. And people around me began to notice the shift, drawn to this vibrant, authentic version of me.

I had a girlfriend at the time, who, perhaps unknowingly, provided an invaluable safe space for me to be fully honest, open, and wholeheartedly myself. The person who had been crying to come out, hidden behind a mask of forced normalcy and ready-made jokes, had finally seen the light of day. The old, suffocating fear of exposure was no longer present. For perhaps the first time in my life, I was 100% me during this period, shedding the protective layers of self-preservation I'd meticulously built over years of quiet, internal suffering.

And because of that radical authenticity, I recognize now, I was inadvertently allowing the very demons I had suppressed to finally surface. The panic attacks and anxiety had been lurking in the shadows of my subconscious, kept at bay by years of enforced control and the desperate, all-consuming need to "be normal." Now, in this period of genuine self-expression and lowered guards, they began to emerge, often at the most inopportune times, but almost exclusively around people I trusted completely, when my defenses were down. They came on fast and quick, sometimes materializing from absolutely nowhere, escalating from zero to one hundred in a terrifying, dizzying rush, instantly pulling me back to the hell I once lived. The familiar physical symptoms – the heart pounding like a drum against my ribs, the desperate struggle for breath, the terrifying numbness spreading through my limbs – they were all back, but now without the clear, external trigger of a looming surgical date.

This ushered in a new, bewildering battle, one I was ill-equipped to fight. Trying desperately to understand the unknown enemy of this new, pervasive anxiety, while simultaneously being terrified of its present, immediate manifestation. To my great dismay, those who couldn't see the unseen wounds started to doubt me. They dismissed these panic attacks as fake, suggesting I was simply drawing attention to myself, as if I craved constant companionship or sympathy. These accusations stung deeply and painfully because no one, absolutely no one, truly knew the silent hell I had already been through, the lifetime of physical and psychological pain that had conditioned my nervous system to a constant state of alert.

The panic attacks became more frequent and intensely strong, leaving me feeling perpetually vulnerable and exposed, always waiting for the next attack. In my desperation for relief, for a momentary reprieve from the relentless internal torment, I found an unexpected, dangerous solace in the calming euphoria of alcohol. I would drink, methodically, deliberately, to calm my frayed nerves, to literally drown out the psychic pain that welled up inside me, the relentless fear that gripped my chest. This "sneaky little devil," as I came to think of it, worked with alarming efficiency. And it worked surprisingly well. In its haze, I found a fleeting sense of grace and joy, a blissful numbness. I genuinely liked how it made me feel – numb to the fear, delightfully disengaged from the gnawing anxiety, temporarily free from the constant, exhausting battle within my own mind and body.

Once my girlfriend at the time ended our relationship, a breakup that inflicted its own emotional wounds, the solace I found in *The Sneaky Devil* intensified exponentially. It became a dual-purpose escape. To calm the hurt and heartbreak of the relationship's end, and to keep the relentless anxiety, now unmoored from the safe harbor of her presence, at bay. I have to admit, with a heavy heart, it did work. And it worked powerfully. I found a manufactured grace and fleeting joy in its oblivion. I liked how I felt, even if I knew, deep down, it was a hollow, unsustainable peace.

10

The Quiet Understanding: A Father's Presence, A Son's Emerging Battle – And a Breakthrough

During this pivotal period, I was living with my dad. A man whose profession as a police officer dictated a demanding schedule of odd, unpredictable working hours, meant I was often left alone, responsible for my own time and decisions. This forced independence, however, wasn't a burden; it was a crucible, shaping me into a more self-reliant individual. I learned to navigate my days with purpose, balancing school, juggling multiple jobs, and managing my own responsibilities, all while soaking in the quiet, unspoken lessons of self-reliance that came from his trust.

Yet, when my dad *was* home, those moments were pure gold. We would talk, and by "talk," I mean truly communicate, to see one another and be seen. Our conversations weren't superficial; they were sprawling, uninhibited explorations of everything and anything that crossed our minds, from the mundane details of our respective days to the deeper currents of life, thoughts, and feelings. I cherished these times with an almost sacred reverence; it was the kind of open, honest relationship I had always longed for with him, a deep, resonant connection. And I instinctively knew, through his patient listening and engaged responses, that he desired it just as much. The more time we spent together, the more deeply we got to know each other, forging a bond that quickly blossomed into the best of friendships. To this day, even after so many years, I can honestly say there's nowhere I'd rather be than simply spending time, just talking, with him.

While living under his roof, surrounded by the unspoken security of his presence, my panic attacks, though still a menacing, lurking presence, were mercifully few and far between. They would occasionally pop up, often terrifying in their sudden, unbidden onset, but usually when I was away from him — at school, at one of my jobs, or just out navigating the world on my own. This left me feeling acutely trapped and isolated inside my own head, a deeply unsettling sensation that scared me as the "unknown" — the true, bewildering nature of these episodes — seemed to surface with greater force each time. Again, the prescription drugs, the Ativan from my family doctor, remained untouched, a small, forgotten bottle gathering dust on a shelf. Little did I realize, in my stubborn, almost phobic fear of their chemical embrace, just how very helpful they would eventually prove to be. The memory of forced sedation, of losing control to the very substances meant to help me, was too strong, too visceral.

Those two amazing, formative years living with my dad flew by in a blur of growth and mutual understanding. Our conversations, as they often did, began to turn to my future, specifically my burning desire to move out on my own, to claim full independence. I was ready, brimming with youthful ambition and a solid, hard-earned work ethic. At the time, I was juggling three demanding jobs: I'd be up at dawn, my hands toughening from hours of landscaping in the mornings; then I'd rush to Quiznos for a two-hour lunch shift, battling the noon-hour chaos; and finally, I'd head to The Keg Steakhouse for evening shifts that often stretched late into the night. Through these experiences, I quickly learned the tangible value of money, the weight of responsibility, and the satisfaction of earned exhaustion. With both a sense of personal readiness and a shared understanding between us, we decided it was time for me to take that next, significant step towards full independence.

Once I moved out, the fragile peace I'd found, the careful equilibrium I'd maintained, began to crumble with alarming speed. My panic attacks returned with a vengeance, no longer content to be few and far between. They would erupt, usually when I wasn't at work, when the structured distraction and focus of responsibility weren't there to hold them at bay. They'd strike when I was at home, trying to unwind with my cousins or friends, moments that should have been relaxing, filled with laughter and easy camaraderie. This concerned me deeply, a cold dread settling in, as they started to become alarmingly frequent and relentlessly strong, each one a terrifying replay of the last. In most cases, their sheer intensity, the overwhelming physical and mental assault, led me to rely on the most drastic measure I knew: calling 911. My calls were driven by genuine, abject terror of the unknown, of a body and mind betraying me. All these terrifying feelings felt precisely as if I was back at the hospital, being prepped for surgery, descending into that familiar, suffocating hell, but I obviously wasn't. The disorienting, horrifying disconnect between my internal experience and external reality, the sense that I was dying from the inside out, convinced me, with every fiber of my being, that these attacks were going to kill me. Each time the sirens wailed, growing closer, I truly believed this might be the last time.

It was during one such desperate 911 call, late at night, that help arrived in the form of an ambulance pulling up to my house, its red and white lights flashing silently against the windows. The paramedic stepped out, with a surprising air of familiarity. He took one look at me, shaking and gasping for breath, and recognized me. He cut straight to the chase, his voice calm but authoritative, asking if I had been prescribed any medication for these episodes. I, of course, admitted that I had, but confessed my paralyzing fear of actually taking it, the old surgical traumas resurfacing at the mere thought.

"What is it?" he asked, his gaze steady, devoid of judgment.

"Xanax," I managed to stammer out, the name feeling foreign on my trembling tongue, correcting my earlier memory of Ativan, though at the moment,
it was all just "the drug."

He looked at me, a young man clinging to the edge of an unseen precipice, and gave me a direct, no-nonsense instruction: "Take it. We'll sit with you right here in the ambulance, and if it doesn't help, if you still feel like this, then we'll go to the hospital. But let's try this first."

So there I was, sitting in the back of the ambulance, the world outside blurred by flashing lights, utterly scared shitless. My heart was still hammering, my hands clammy, about to take a drug I was terrified to consume, a substance I didn't truly understand, only knew as something that altered consciousness. I remember the pill felt tiny, insignificant, yet held the weight of all my fears. I placed it on my tongue, swallowed it with a dry, trembling gulp, and felt it go into my system, bracing myself for whatever might come, for the familiar disassociation, the loss of control. With a voice barely a whisper, thick with fear and a strange sense of surrender, I confessed to the paramedics, "This is the first time I've ever used it."

The next twenty minutes crawled by, each second a torturous eternity of waiting, of hyper-awareness of every internal sensation. Then, subtly at first, a remarkable shift began. I noticed the drug began to work its magic. The suffocating, iron grip of my anxiety and panic began to loosen, then dissolve entirely, as if an invisible hand had wiped away the past two hours of terror. The racing thoughts quieted, my breath deepened, and the tremor in my limbs ceased. He looked at me, a gentle, knowing smile spreading across his face, and said, "See? I told you Xanax works for anxiety and panic attacks."

Dumbfounded by the rapid, almost miraculous relief, of the silence that had fallen over my internal storm, and profoundly thankful, I could only nod. I thanked the paramedics profusely as they quietly gathered their equipment and left. I walked back into my house, the lingering fear replaced by a quiet awe and a cautious hope, and offered a weak, genuine smile at my cousins, who had been watching from the doorway, their faces etched with deep concern.

"I'm okay," I said, the words feeling true, finally. A wave of relief washed over their expressions as they saw the storm had passed. It was a pivotal moment, a forced step into a new, terrifying, yet ultimately liberating understanding of my own internal landscape. For the first time, I had a weapon, not against a surgeon's knife, but against the insidious attacks of my own mind.

11

The Fortress of My Twenties: Building a Life, Keeping the Past at Bay

My twenties were a decade defined by an intense focus on living, on actively constructing a life that felt entirely, deliberately separate from the deep shadows of my childhood. It wasn't a period characterized by confronting my past, or by peeling back the intricate, painful layers of old wounds. Instead, it was about erecting an elaborate inner wall, a complex psychological fortress designed with a singular, overriding purpose: to keep the younger, more vulnerable version of myself, with all his accompanying pain, fear, and unresolved trauma, firmly at bay. Looking back now, from the vantage point of thirty-nine, I can clearly see the intricate architecture of that wall. A precise, almost unconscious, blend of denial, avoidance, and a relentless, almost obsessive, focus on the immediate, tangible present. Every achievement, every social gathering, every carefully curated moment served as another brick in that protective barrier.

The Sneaky Devil, by then, had seamlessly woven itself into the fabric of my existence, becoming an integral, almost unquestioned, part of my daily and social routine. It wasn't a destructive force in the typical sense, not a chaotic descent into the stereotypical abyss of addiction that people often envision. Instead, it was a constant, steady current that flowed smoothly through my social life, an ever-present companion. It served as a remarkably effective tool, a social lubricant that allowed me to navigate complex social situations with an effortless ease, to feel comfortable, confident, and utterly at home in my own skin, even when underlying anxieties might have otherwise screamed in protest. And, perhaps most significantly, it acted as a powerful, reliable sedative, consistently keeping the insidious tendrils of panic attacks firmly at bay, deep beneath the surface.

The panic attacks, once a frequent and terrifying ordeal that had gripped my adolescence with a visceral intensity, became distant echoes, faint whispers in the background of my life. They rarely surfaced, perhaps once every six months if I was unlucky, sometimes even years apart, mere fleeting shadows of a past torment. The relief from their absence was palpable, a liberation that allowed me to live without the constant, gnawing fear of an impending attack. It was a freedom I savored, believing I had somehow outgrown or conquered them. I was, in a way, living a double life: outwardly, I was the undisputed life of the party, the effervescent social butterfly, seemingly without a care in the world, always ready with a joke or a plan. Inwardly, however, I was still carrying the immense, unresolved weight of my past, albeit unknowingly. I truly believed I had simply moved beyond it, that time and a certain amount of self-medication had been enough to heal all wounds.

Then, at a time when I was so comfortable, so entrenched within my carefully constructed world, I met my wife. Our relationship began organically, not with grand gestures, but as a genuine, uncomplicated friendship, a foundation built on shared laughter, easy companionship, and countless late-night conversations that stretched into the early hours, peeling back layers of personality. She possessed an uncanny ability to see me for who I truly was, the good, the bad, and everything in between, without flinching. She witnessed my moments of brilliance, my flashes of unexpected vulnerability, and even the subtle cracks in my meticulously constructed facade, the carefully chosen jokes and performances I used to deflect and protect.

She quickly became more than just a friend. She was a true *confidante*, a genuine safe haven where, for the first time, I could finally begin to be myself, without pretense, without the crippling fear of judgment that had always haunted me. Slowly, gently, patiently, she learned about my past: the childhood traumas that had shaped my earliest years, the lingering anxiety that still simmered beneath my confident exterior, and the quiet, almost subconscious reliance on alcohol as my primary, unacknowledged coping mechanism. But crucially, she didn't judge. She listened with an open heart, she understood with a depth and empathy I hadn't encountered before, and she accepted me for who I was, flaws and all. Her acceptance was a warmth that began to melt the ice around my guarded heart.

In her steady, unwavering presence, the inner wall I had so painstakingly built over two decades began to crumble, brick by brick. It wasn't a sudden collapse, but a gradual erosion. The distant echoes of my past, once so faint they were almost imperceptible, grew louder, more insistent, demanding to be heard, to be acknowledged, to finally be felt. The memories, once neatly compartmentalized, started to bleed into my conscious thoughts. But despite this undeniable internal shift, I was still deeply reluctant to confront them head-on, to actively dismantle the fortress that had, for so long, paradoxically both protected and imprisoned me. I was comfortable in my denial, content to live perpetually in the present, still oblivious, or perhaps willfully blind, to the ticking time bomb of unresolved trauma that lay buried beneath the comforting rubble of my past. It was a comfortable lie, and I clung to it, even as the first tremors of its eventual collapse began to shake my carefully ordered world.

The friendship my wife and I shared, already a bedrock of laughter, easy companionship, and countless late-night talks, deepened effortlessly into a loving, committed relationship. We started dating, a natural progression, and as I also got to peeled back the layers of her world, her hopes, her dreams, her intricate past, she, in turn, discovered the often-guarded complexities of mine. The level of trust that blossomed between us was unlike anything I had ever known, a palpable, almost sacred force that seemed to bind us irrevocably. It wasn't just a feeling. It was a deep, mutual understanding, a shared certainty that made future steps inevitable. Marriage, just two years into our journey together, became less a question to be pondered and more an obvious, joyful certainty we both embraced without hesitation.

My anxiety, though still a familiar part of my internal landscape, was a rarity during those years of early adulthood and new love. It would occasionally pop up, a fleeting shadow across my inner peace, a brief, unsettling ripple. But my wife was always there, an unwavering presence. She'd stand by me every step of the way, her presence a quiet anchor, grounding me with a gentle touch or a softly spoken word, patiently guiding me back to reality from the edge of those internal storms. There was never any judgment in her eyes, just earnest understanding, and a calm assurance that allowed me to weather those moments, knowing I wasn't alone or misunderstood.

As my twenties drew to a close, a new life entered our world. Our son was born. He was a tiny, utterly dependent being, a culmination of love, connection, and the weight of new responsibility. The moment I held him, a fierce protectiveness swelled within me. Before his arrival, I had firmly declared, both to myself and my wife, that I would quit alcohol. The thought of him viewing me, his father, through the haze of my drinking, even if it was merely to fall asleep, felt fundamentally wrong. It wasn't the image I wanted to project, nor the example I wished to set for this precious new life.

Unfortunately, the demanding reality of my job made this resolve incredibly difficult to maintain. My shifts were a constant, unpredictable dance across the clock, demanding that I be available at any hour of the day or night. One week I might be on days, the next on nights, then a swing shift that left my internal clock in disarray. The Sneaky Devil, I realized with a creeping sense of inevitability, had become deeply ingrained in my sleep routine. It wasn't about getting drunk, or even about socializing or partying; it was purely functional, a desperate measure. It helped me shut off my mind, to quiet the growing clamor of a new, specific kind of anxiety that now haunted me— the intense pressure to perform well at work.

The thought of not being able to fall asleep the night before a crucial, demanding shift, of that directly impacting my performance and potentially jeopardizing my employment, was a paralyzing terror. I was so nervous about the prospect of losing my job, of not being able to adequately support my burgeoning family, that the drinking continued, almost without conscious thought, a desperate, silent bargain with myself. It was a means to an end, a desperate measure to maintain stability in a world that now had infinitely higher stakes.

Life settled into a predictable rhythm, a quiet routine that felt comfortable, almost stagnant in its predictability, but safe. My anxiety would still pop its head in and out every now and then, a quick, unsettling appearance like a fleeting ghost, but I had a reliable tool now. I would reach for the Xanax when the panic attacks flared, swallowing the small pill that brought an almost miraculous calm, pulling me back from the brink of internal chaos. Things, it seemed, were under control for a few years.

The fortress I had built around my past, a monument to denial and avoidance, remained largely intact. It was reinforced by the comforting predictability of routine, the deep, abiding love of my growing family, and the quiet, nightly presence of The Sneaky Devil, complemented by medication as an emergency brake. I was managing, surviving, and existing within the careful boundaries I had drawn for myself.

12

The Unraveling: Covid, Loss, and a Confrontation with Self

My late thirties, a period that should have been defined by an established routine and family life, instead became a subtle unraveling, a slow but undeniable dismantling of the inner wall I had so painstakingly built. For years, my anxiety and panic had largely been under control, reduced to infrequent, unpredictable pop-ups, managed by a precise combination of routine, avoidance, and the quiet assistance of *The Sneaky Devil* or Xanax.

Then, COVID hit. For my family and me, the pandemic was a unique experience, layered with its own peculiar stresses. My wife and I, embarking on a major life change, had finally received approval for a significant house renovation and extension precisely when COVID was at its most intense. We were plunged into total lockdown, navigating a world where, at times, it was literally illegal to even be outside. Looking back, that feels utterly wild to comprehend, a surreal chapter in collective memory. We moved into a rental unit, living amidst boxes and temporary arrangements while our home became a construction zone.

My alcohol use during this period, probably mirroring many others, was heavy at times. I knew it was problematic, marking a distinct departure from my usual functional drinking. The sheer boredom of lockdown, with nothing to do but endlessly replay video games, led me to drink primarily to "have fun," to make the monotonous days go by faster. And it definitely did. So, when the call came to return to work, I welcomed it like a lifeline, thanking the heavens for the return of purpose.

My job as a flight attendant manager brought me into a completely different, often volatile, environment. The pandemic, it seemed, had unleashed a wave of disruptive passengers, the kind you'd see going viral on TikTok or YouTube – grown adults throwing tantrums, acting like uneducated, disrespectful children. My primary role was to support the flight attendants, ensuring their aircraft remained safe and their authority upheld. Despite the challenges, I absolutely loved my job. I loved coming into work, speaking with the employees, being present with them, supporting them. It gave me a new perspective, an unwavering respect for what flight attendants endured daily.

My alcohol use, once back at work, reverted to its former, more "normal" state: primarily used just to fall asleep, a functional tool to quiet the mind after demanding shifts. Once COVID began to recede, and life started its slow, often awkward, return to "normal"—or rather, its "new normal"—events began to unfold as nature intended, pushing me further into the complexities of adulthood.

My grandmother, on my mother's side, began to develop onset dementia, slowly but undeniably declining in her health and faculties. One day, she suffered a fall, breaking her hip, which confined her to a wheelchair.

I visited her in early October. The air in her room was heavy with the quiet progression of her illness. As I sat with her, she looked at me with a gaze that flickered between recognition and confusion.

"Matt," she said, her voice thin, "you have no hair, you look so different without hair." A strange, almost out-of-body sensation washed over me. I had lost my hair when I was 19; I was 36 then. That single, seemingly innocuous sentence, spoken by someone whose mind was unmoored from the present, allowed me to fully accept a reality I had long dismissed with humor or deflection: yes, it's real, and yes, it's happening. The physical changes brought on by time, which I had so easily dismissed, were now undeniable. I left that day with a concerned eyebrow raised for her, my thoughts of her throughout my life swirling around my head a million times over, a kaleidoscope of cherished memories and the painful realization of her decline.

December 26th would be the last day I would ever see her alive. She had lost an alarming amount of weight and muscle; she must have weighed maybe 80 pounds. Her jaw muscles were barely intact, making speech for her incredibly difficult, each word a monumental effort. Her dementia was now at 100%; my mom had pre-warned me that she might not recognize me, cautioning me not to be scared, not to take it personally.

I sat with her for about ten minutes, the silence punctuated by her shallow breaths. Initially, I could feel her soul wasn't entirely present; her eyes were unfocused, distant. But then, a sudden, piercing gaze locked with mine. For a brief, precious moment, she snapped back into her body, her eyes alight with recognition.

"Oh, hi Matt," she whispered, a fragile smile gracing her lips. "Thanks for coming over."

She asked how my wife and son were doing, as she always did, even when they weren't there, a testament to her enduring love. And of course, with that glimmer of her old self, she always added, her voice filled with a familiar pride, that she was proud of me. She knew the struggles I had gone through, the battles I had fought, and I knew I held a special, unique place in her heart.

A beautiful and fascinating thing happened as we said goodbye. When my brother and I were kids visiting her and my grandfather, she would always say goodbye to us in a different language—sometimes French, sometimes Italian, sometimes Japanese, a playful ritual. As I was leaving that small, dim room where she lay helpless, completely vulnerable, she looked at me directly in my eyes, a final, lucid spark of connection. And she said, "Sayonara."

I knew, with a certainty that chilled me to the bone, that this was the last time I would ever see her. She died a week later.

I had an important exam to write the day after I saw her. A crucial turning point for me. I decided then, with a new, fierce resolve, that I wasn't going to drink any alcohol. I needed to be completely sober, clear-headed, not hung over, and fully present for that exam, as it was vitally important to me, a step towards a new professional chapter. I, of course, passed this exam and carried on with my job, the external world continuing its demands.

When I got the call saying she had passed away, my initial, gut reaction was a stark, unvarnished thought: *Fuck! This is not good.* And then, a more assured, deliberate decision cemented itself. I decided I wasn't going to drink any alcohol. Not one drop. I needed to feel the grief, to allow the raw emotions to wash over me naturally, without hiding any feelings from myself, without numbing the pain. I wanted to completely, utterly *feel* her death, to experience the full weight of this great loss. The wall, though still standing, was about to face its first true, unmitigated emotional assault.

In the immediate aftermath of my grandmother's passing, a shift occurred. Amidst the raw, unmediated grief I had deliberately chosen to feel, an unexpected outlet emerged: *the gym.* It was an almost primal calling, a need to channel the torrent of emotion into something tangible, something that promised control and transformation. I set a concrete goal: from a lean 138 lbs, I aimed for 170 lbs of solid muscle. My entire focus narrowed to this physical quest, a deliberate path to learn how to feel, how to truly heal, not just from the loss, but from the cumulative weight of my past.

My first day in the gym was a visceral experience. Each lift, each strained muscle fiber, felt like an active engagement with the emotions of losing my grandmother. It wasn't just physical exertion; it was an emotional release. In that new environment, pushing my body to its limits, I felt better, more connected with myself, a sense of quiet contentment and burgeoning power. Crucially, I noticed something remarkable: I wasn't craving alcohol. The familiar urge to numb or escape was replaced by the invigorating burn of effort. My routine fundamentally shifted, from drinking to induce sleep and quiet my mind, to the disciplined ritual of weightlifting. I began to feel better about myself, my mind clearer, a burgeoning sense of happiness and confidence taking root.

Just three months after my grandmother's death, my mom called, her voice tinged with a familiar gravity. My grandfather had suffered a stroke and was in the hospital. The message was clear: now was the best time to see him, as they didn't know how much longer he would be able to hold on.

My brother and sister-in-law drove me to the hospital. The atmosphere in his room was somber, heavy with the weight of unspoken goodbyes. My uncle, aunt, and cousins surrounded his bed, their faces visibly upset. They quietly informed us that he was unable to talk or move, semi-conscious, a shadow of the man he once was. My aunt and uncle graciously stepped out, allowing my brother and me a private moment with him. Even through the damage his body had sustained, you could see he was still present, his eyes, though clouded, were able to scan the room and recognize us, a flicker of his sharp mind remaining. My brother spoke first, his voice thick with emotion.

Then, it was my turn. I leaned over his bed, our eyes meeting, and a strange, poignant thought came to me, a desperate attempt to bring a touch of levity to the crushing sorrow.

"Grandad," I began, my voice softer than I intended, "isn't life weird? How when I was a kid, you and Nana would always come visit me while I was laying in bed recovering from surgery? And here we are now, it's me visiting you while you lay recovering? Total 180, eh?"

I tried to infuse kindness into the words, to make him feel seen, to acknowledge our shared, unique history. And then, a miracle. From the depths of the damage in his brain, from a body seemingly stripped of all agency, he let out an incredible, genuine laugh. A wide, beautiful smile spread across his face, a momentary beacon of his old self. In that laugh, in that smile, I heard a lifetime of love, resilience, and connection. I knew, with a certainty that settled deep in my bones, that this was the last time I would ever see him. A week later, he too, would pass away.

The same initial emotions that had gripped me with my grandmother's death ran through my body: that hot, tingling sensation, that mind-numbing reality that someone important was no longer with us. My grandparents, both of them, had cared so deeply about my brother and me. They were tender-hearted people, true salt of the earth, who had envisioned and worked tirelessly for a better life for their children and grandchildren. Immigrants from England, they had raised a family in Canada through sheer hard work and sharp intellect, embodying a quiet strength. My only regret, a persistent ache, was not spending more time with them in their later years, though life's demands and long drives on the highway stuck in traffic everytime had made regular visits incredibly difficult.

This time, with my grandfather's passing, I could have easily used it as an excuse to fall back into alcohol, to numb the pain of this second massive loss in such a short period. But I specifically chose not to. My focus remained steadfast on my weight goal at the gym. I needed to feel the grief, to allow the emotion to wash over me, to genuinely connect with myself in those raw moments. I needed to be more present, to not hide from the pain, but to embrace it as part of the process.

And something in my core clicked. In the disciplined pursuit of physical strength, in the conscious embrace of grief, I was able to be more present, more authentically myself. The person who had so briefly emerged at 18, filled with that fierce sense of "NO!" but with a newfound authenticity. With this deeper connection to my emotions, came an unwelcome resurgence. It was as if by dismantling the old walls, I had reopened a door. What was that lurking presence, now bolder and more frequent? **Panic.** One, two, three panic attacks within a single month. The dormant beast had awakened, seemingly stronger than ever.

Part Three

13

The Fortress Crumbles: When Safety Zones Collapse and Truth Demands to Be Heard

The immeasurable loss of my grandparents, two bedrock figures in my life, and my conscious, deliberate decision to embrace that grief without alcohol's numbing veil, had inadvertently triggered a new, terrifying phase in my life.

Amidst the raw, unmediated sorrow I had chosen to feel, my mind became a relentless, chaotic battlefield of overthinking. I desperately spun in a dizzying spiral, trying to make sense of the sudden, unbidden resurgence of panic attacks, searching for logical explanations, for solutions, but coming up with nothing but more questions.

In a desperate, almost primal attempt to regain some semblance of control over this internal chaos, I mentally mapped out "safe spaces"—specific locations where I believed I wouldn't have panic attacks. These carefully designated sanctuaries were: the familiar comfort of my home, the structured environment of my workplace, and the invigorating discipline of the gym. For a significant period, this fragile strategy seemed to hold. The attacks, though now disturbingly regular, consistently avoided these zones, erupting seemingly out of the blue but never within the self-imposed boundaries of my perceived safety. I clung to this illusion of control, believing I had outsmarted the beast.

Until one day, the illusion shattered. I was at work, a place I loved, a place where I felt competent, present, and useful. Suddenly, as I approached the bustling airport security checkpoint, an overwhelming feeling of danger, pain, suffering, and fear washed over me. It wasn't a physical barrier, but an invisible wall, an impenetrable, suffocating psychological barrier. I felt, with absolute certainty, that if I dared to step through that security gate, the terror would only intensify, consuming me entirely, leaving me exposed and helpless. I couldn't bear to be in the public eye, surrounded by strangers, vulnerable to this internal onslaught. I instinctively retreated, my legs moving on their own, seeking refuge in a quiet, forgotten corner—a tucked-away spot where I used to sit during the early COVID lockdowns when I wasn't laid off, letting the monotonous days pass. Here, in this makeshift haven, far from the critical gaze of others, I allowed myself to sink into the full force of the physical sensations: the racing heart, the constricted throat, the desperate struggle for air, the relentless torrent of negative thoughts, the overwhelming, terrifying feeling of complete loss of control. These sensations were boldly present, intensely strong, pushing me to my absolute limit. This was also the first time I felt the chilling sensation of dissociation with such overwhelming force, a terrifying disconnect from my body and my surroundings that, while vaguely familiar from the hazy memories of childhood surgeries, had never manifested with this raw, undeniable power. It was like watching myself from outside my own body, detached and terrified.

A text message from a friend, a colleague on break, asking where I was, sliced through the fog of my terror, bringing me back to a sliver of awareness. I managed to text back, "I'm having a panic attack." She found me quickly, her face etched with profound concern, and wordlessly brought me a warm cup of tea. Though she was doing her absolute best to try and help me, her efforts felt tragically futile against the tidal wave of anxiety and panic that had reached a new, incomprehensible height. Once she left, unable to break through my mental prison, I did something utterly unprecedented: I Googled a crisis hotline, my fingers trembling on the phone, and spoke to someone, my voice raw and broken as I tried to articulate the incomprehensible chaos within me. It was the first time I had ever sought external help for my internal suffering.

This singular, terrifying panic attack at work didn't just disrupt my day; it opened the floodgates, irrevocably changing the trajectory of my mental state. I now possessed an undeniable, terrifying clarity: my decades of alcohol use, which I had so meticulously controlled and rationalized, had been nothing more than a powerful mask, a deceptive shield. It had diligently hidden, suppressed, and numbed what had been trying to come out all those years ago—the unexpressed fear, terror, and searing pain of the young child who had endured so much, now finally surging back into the present with an undeniable force.

For the first time ever, at 37 years old, I started therapy. I was cautious, even skeptical, but open. Yet, with the therapist's deep knowledge and deeper empathy, coupled with my new, unyielding willingness to finally open up—to truly speak my truth—we connected unbelievably well right from the first session. Through our conversations, we quickly recognized the core truth: It was the *younger version of myself*, the scared child on the gurney, the boy enduring repeated trauma, expressing the very fear, terror, and pain that I had hidden so meticulously as a child, now finally surging back into the present. The goal became clear, daunting but necessary: to allow these long-suppressed emotions to come out, to feel them fully, and to learn to manage them as they arose, rather than instinctively suppressing them, as I had done for so long. Crucially, I was now finally connected with myself in an almost spiritual way, fully aware of my internal landscape, feeling truly safe with my therapist, and 100% committed to combating this. I yearned for clarity, for lasting peace of mind, and for the unwavering belief that, eventually, it would all be okay.

As the months of therapy progressed, a new opportunity arose within my company, and I made the difficult decision to move to a different position. I will *always* miss my job as a flight attendant manager, and I will forever love every single person I worked with in that role. It was a fulfilling chapter, filled with camaraderie and purpose. But I knew, deep down, that I needed a significant change, primarily for myself and my ongoing healing journey. The new role provided exactly what I needed: the tools and resources to focus inwardly, to continue my personal work, and surprisingly, it also empowered me to extend that support and understanding to others. The team was composed of amazing individuals, compassionate and understanding, and I loved them dearly for the new environment they provided.

I became increasingly vocal about the struggles I was going through, a new level of vulnerability that would have been utterly unthinkable in my earlier years. Yet, I always made sure to reassure my colleagues that my personal battles wouldn't interfere with my work. That part of my brain, I found, remained surprisingly separate, efficient even amidst turmoil, a testament to years of compartmentalization. And, critically, work itself had once again become a safe space for me, a place of structure and purpose, filled with people I trusted, who, in turn, trusted me unconditionally.

But as my deep dives into therapy continued, a perplexing pattern began to emerge about the nature of my panic attacks. I started to recognize that they were occurring, almost exclusively, around people of trust. Whether it was with my beloved wife on a peaceful vacation, or with my mom atop a beautiful mountain trail, with my dad at his home, at a bustling restaurant with friends, or with my son at a soccer game – the physical location no longer mattered. The attacks were now directly, inextricably linked to the presence of my most trustworthy, most cherished people.

The reason, as my therapist and I uncovered, was both heartbreaking and liberating: Because I trust these people so fully, their presence instinctively lowered my internal guard, disarming the deeply ingrained blocks and threat levels I've maintained for decades as a survival mechanism. In allowing myself to feel more vulnerable, the raw, unfiltered emotions and trauma within me finally got to scream out, as if a younger, trapped voice inside is desperately yelling: **"THIS IS WHAT HAPPENED TO ME! I NEED YOU TO LISTEN! I NEED YOU TO HELP ME!"**

I vividly remembered screaming that silently in my head, and sometimes desperately out loud in my terror, as a kid on the gurney, pleading to be saved from the inevitable operating room. But back then, the brutal reality was, surgery was still going to happen. I was still going to go into that hell, alone. Now, these panic attacks were a desperate, delayed cry for the help I couldn't receive then.

Now, when that anxiousness begins to set in, when the familiar physical sensations of panic start to take hold, I feel these sensations harder and harder, where it would be so overwhelmingly intense that I now recognize I *need* to tell someone, to actively lean on them for support. That, for me, was completely foreign territory—a weakness I had long denied myself, a vulnerability I had fiercely guarded. The very first step was calling that crisis hotline and getting set up with a therapist, who, right off the bat, I connected with incredibly well, a crucial lifeline. The second, and perhaps most liberating, step was finally talking about it, acknowledging, truly acknowledging, not just to myself but to another human being, that I was dealing with something so gravely traumatic from my past.

I finally accepted support. I wholly believed in its power, in its necessity. And once I fully accepted it, once I dropped the last vestiges of my protective armor, once I committed to truly feeling and healing, unknowingly, my panic attacks became even more *frequent* and *stronger*. It was a terrifying paradox: the path to healing seemed to first lead deeper into the very pain I sought to escape. The fortress was not just crumbling; it was being actively, intentionally dismantled, and all the raw, powerful, terrifying contents that had been locked away for so long were finally, irrevocably, spilling out into the abyss.

January 2025. The plan was simple: escape the Toronto chill, soak up some sun, and to at last, fully enjoy a birthday trip without the shadow of a panic attack. The bonus? My flight attendant friends, the ones who'd become family through countless airport skirmishes and shared anxieties, random humour and mental passenger stories, had pulled strings to be on my flight. Our bond, forged in the crucible of unpredictable travel and early morning support calls, felt unbreakable. That team of friends working my flight home was more exciting than the destination itself.

Landing in the heat, the tropical air a balm on my skin, the resort beckoned.
But all things can't be good can they? The messages came in: my cousin, who to this day is still my best friend. Then the phone call from my dad. *My uncle was gone.* Cancer. Just like that. He

was more than my father's brother; he was another steadfast anchor in my chaotic twenties, the one who'd pulled me back from my deepest rock bottom. He was a force of nature, fiercely loving his son, my best friend. My cousin and I, inseparable in our youth, always chose family. That was his legacy – a monolithic, unwavering presence that now left a gaping hole.

There I was, The Sneaky Devil woke up, the siren song of self-medication whispering in my ear. The old me, the one I desperately wanted to leave behind, would have drowned the grief, convinced it was the path to a "good time." But this time, something was different. I clung to my goal, to the newfound clarity that screamed, "Don't go back there!" Instead, I spent hours on the phone with my cousin. We peeled back every layer – the good, the bad, the terrifying uncertainty of the future. Nothing was left unsaid. The trip, against all odds, became a triumph. Moments of anxiety flickered, yes, but they were quickly extinguished by the warmth of the sun and the sheer determination to stay present.

14

The Panic Unleashed

The flight home wasn't just a journey; it was the gateway. The moment my younger self, the one I thought I'd finally shed, saw a glimmer of light and surged forward, dragging me back into the very darkness I'd fought so hard to escape.

Twenty minutes after takeoff, it hit. Not a gradual onset, but a terrifying, immediate numbness in my hands. This wasn't the pre-flight jitters I knew; this was zero to one hundred in an instant. My friend, the same flight attendant from the inbound flight, was there. I caught her eye, a desperate plea passed between us, and quietly told her I was in the grip of a powerful panic attack. I knew the rules, the safety protocols, the criteria for an emergency landing. I knew I didn't meet them, and I certainly didn't want to alarm other passengers.

I spoke calmly, explaining the situation, stressing that if it worsened, the pilots needed to know. The pilot, surprisingly, came out. I assured him, drawing on my past experience as an inflight manager, that I was fully aware, and for now, I had it "under control."

"Under control" was a lie my lips formed while my mind screamed. My wife, who was at home, my other flight attendant friend who'd dropped me off, also at home, the friend on the flight, and my mother who was in florida– a relentless tag team of texts – desperately tried to keep me from the edge. My friend, further back on the plane, trapped in his seat, knew my distress but trusted I was in capable hands.

Those capable hands belonged to the four women who formed a fragile shelter against the coming storm. I swallowed one and a half Xanax, a desperate gamble, but the rising tide of panic barely acknowledged it. The flight stretched on for five and a half agonizing hours. By the time we landed, my body was a hollowed-out shell. I had so little energy left once I got home, that my wife's embrace was the only thing holding me upright. She led me upstairs, and I fell into a 24-hour blackout of exhaustion.

This wasn't a panic attack I'd ever known. This was different, deeper. It had cracked open a door, unleashing a new, more potent breed of terror. Each subsequent attack would grow stronger, more relentless, pushing me further into an unfamiliar abyss.

15

The False Calm and the Resurgent Terror

Months passed, a quiet stretch of what I mistakenly believed was normalcy. The debilitating panic attacks seemed to have vanished, a cruel illusion. I celebrated this small, personal victory, sharing my newfound calmness with a few close friends, basking in the glow of what felt like a hard-won triumph. A sense of relief, even confidence, swelled within me. I genuinely believed I had it under control, that the "big one" I'd endured on the flight was an anomaly, and the next one was a distant, barely imaginable worry.

Just a week after my confident pronouncements, the insidious tendrils of panic began their return. It started with a subtle tremor, a familiar, unsettling unease while out with family at a bustling restaurant. It was manageable, so I kept it to myself, a secret dread. The dissociation returned, strong and swift, momentarily pulling me from the familiar world, making the vibrant restaurant feel distant, unreal. But a jolt of adrenaline, a primal surge, snapped me back. I immediately deployed the breathing techniques I'd painstakingly learned in therapy, and the wave, mercifully, subsided. I played it off like it was nothing, a minor blip, but the subtle attacks continued, now with alarming regularity, almost weekly. Thankfully, they hadn't yet dared to invade my workplace.

16

The Breaking Point at Work: A Public Unraveling

The calm before another record-breaking storm. It started as a perfectly regular morning. I walked into my office, ready to set up for the day, and decided to grab a customary tea. I asked a friend, a colleague I deeply respected, if she wanted to join me. "I feel kinda off," I admitted to her as we walked down the bustling corridor, a vague premonition swirling in my gut. And then, standing in line, surrounded by the mundane chatter of colleagues, it hit. It was the strongest sensation of dissociation I'd ever experienced, a complete rupture from reality. I felt myself floating, observing, detached. "I think I'm having a panic attack," I mumbled to her, the words feeling foreign and inadequate as they left my lips. It was subtle at first, just enough for me to gather myself and make it back to the relative sanctuary of my office, away from the echoing noise and fluorescent lights.

My friend, understanding the unspoken urgency in my voice, left me to myself but checked in periodically, her presence a quiet reassurance. I hadn't said anything to anyone else; the deep-seated urge to avoid drawing attention to myself was still strong. I called my wife, desperately trying to sound composed, informing her that I was having a "controllable" panic attack, assuring her that if I hadn't gone off the deep end by now, I probably wouldn't.

Boy, was I wrong. My thoughts, instead of engaging with the grounding techniques I'd practiced, fixated relentlessly on my physical symptoms. Every technique, every calming breath, every mental anchor I'd been taught vanished as if wiped clean from a slate. My thoughts instantly made everything worse, spiraling into a terrifying echo chamber of dread. I sent a terse, urgent message to my boss: "Having a bad one."

At that moment, my friend returned, pulling up a chair and sitting with me, offering a steady stream of quiet reassurance. Then, my boss, another trusted friend, came down to my office. Surrounded by these two women, individuals I trusted completely, I let my guard down entirely. I let the panic come to life, uninhibited. It escalated with a terrifying, relentless speed. My physical symptoms became a horrifying mirror of those traumatic episodes from my younger years, when I had absolutely no control: *uncontrollable trembling, cold sweats, a heart hammering a frantic rhythm against my ribs, a relentless barrage of negative, self-annihilating thoughts, pure, unadulterated fear,* **sheer terror**. They got a firsthand, unfiltered look at one of my most terrible attacks.

It was so strong, so utterly overwhelming, that the only solution I could grasp onto was the one I used to turn to in my darkest moments: call EMS. I took my Xanax, but what I truly craved was the mental clarity, the trusted, undeniable authority of the paramedics. Their presence, I knew, would banish all self-doubt, all terrifying questions about my sanity. My friends, their hands tightly gripping mine, did their absolute best to calm me, their words a soothing balm in the maelstrom. And, slowly, agonizingly, I managed to come down from the impossible, soul-crushing attack I had just endured.

In that moment of raw, utterly exposed vulnerability, surrounded by their unwavering kindness and support, I felt a deepening respect for these two women. They were *there*. That was the biggest, most crucial thing. They were there to support me, not out of obligation, but because they genuinely cared. My other work friend, seeing the scene, came into the office and offered his grace and quiet care. I recognized, and truly believed in that moment, for the first time in what felt like forever, that I was surrounded by people who genuinely cared for me. EMS arrived as I was finally calming down, and even through the haze of terror, I expressed my unwavering respect and gratitude for their profession, for their calm efficiency. Now, the drugs finally kicking in, I could feel the terror and fear slowly dissolving, minute by agonizing minute, allowing me to gradually ground myself and settle back into reality.

My wife called back, having been at work, as I had been texting her throughout the ordeal, asking if she could come pick me up and bring me home. She, of course, dropped everything, leaving work immediately to collect her battered, defeated husband. The drive home was a blur of emotional exhaustion. My mind and body, utterly ravaged and spent by the relentless assault, felt empty. Adrenaline gone, energy completely drained, the drugs swirling in a heavy, disorienting high. We got home, and I collapsed into bed. It was probably about noon. I think I only woke up to come downstairs for dinner around 6 PM, a brief, dreamlike interlude before I slipped back upstairs and slept for another 14 hours.

17

A Leave of Absence and the Harrowing Trial of Healing

I called in sick the day after that traumatic panic attack at the airport. I needed a single day to recover, to gather my thoughts and reclaim some semblance of physical energy. It was a day of quiet stillness I ate, I slept, I just relaxed. It was a luxury

I hadn't realized I desperately needed, a small but vital act of self-care that felt both alien and necessary. In my mind, this brief respite was all I needed to hit the "reset" button. I convinced myself I was ready to go back to work the following day and, with a stubborn refusal to fully acknowledge my fragility, I didn't call in sick.

I walked into the office the next morning, exhausted but mentally braced for a difficult conversation. I still clung to the belief that my struggles weren't as dire as my superiors would likely believe. I figured I could just power through it, just as I had always powered through everything else. I sat down with my bosses, the familiar scent of coffee and printer paper filling the air, and we discussed the possibility of a leave. They spoke with care and genuine concern, outlining the resources available to me. Even then, at that moment, I didn't think it was necessary, figuring that if I did take a leave, it wouldn't be for more than a week at most. But their collective wisdom, their clear-eyed view of my state, eventually broke through my resistance. By the end of the workday, I had reluctantly accepted their advice and the assurances they offered. I appreciated both of them for the amount of respect and courtesy they showed, treating me not as a liability, but as a person in need.I called my doctor's office immediately and booked an appointment to get all the paperwork started.

The next day, I sat in his office and explained everything. My doctor listened intently, his face etched with concern as I described the panic attack at work. "Maybe it's time we try and take antidepressants to help you manage these attacks, as they're getting worse and more frequent," he said, his voice gentle but firm. Hearing those words felt like a punch to the gut. It was a confirmation of my deepest fears and a brutal reminder of my firm aversion to drugs. I knew, as I had mentioned so many times before, that I hated the way they made me feel, the loss of control, the hazy disconnect, the physical sense of not being myself.

I left his office with the prescription note in my hand. It sat on my kitchen counter for five agonizing days, a tangible symbol of my internal debate. I was on the fence, paralyzed by the thought of taking them.

Then, on the fifth night, as I was getting ready for bed, the anxiety struck. It shot through my body with the same terrifying speed as the one in my office, a few short days ago. The physical sensations grew strong. Fast. "I don't feel right," I managed to say to my wife as a sense of panic now set in. My heart pounded against my ribs, a frantic drumbeat. My thoughts became dark, all the mental tools I had worked so hard to build and manage became invisible, erased. A tremor began, shaking my entire body uncontrollably, as violently as someone having a seizure. And then, a searing lightning bolt struck in my head, a blinding snap that left me unable to understand who I was anymore. My reality didn't exist at that moment.

I started screaming to my wife, "I DON'T KNOW WHAT'S HAPPENING ANYMORE! I DON'T KNOW WHAT'S HAPPENING!" I was in my own bedroom, but I couldn't recognize it. The memories of my entire life were erased, a terrifying blank. This struck a fear in me that allowed the panic to get to its absolute strongest point. I know I keep saying that each one was the strongest, but it's true. Each one had become progressively stronger, harder to overcome, and this one was a shattering breaking point. My wife got me a Xanax, and within thirty minutes, the storm began to settle. It was about 2 a.m. before I felt fully back in my body, my sense of self returning from the void.

In that moment of quiet clarity, I said to my wife, "Maybe I should take the medication that the doctor prescribed because I can't live like this anymore. They are too hard. I can't mentally handle them."

The next day was a carbon copy of the others following an attack, exhausted, broken down, and just down on myself. I stayed inside all day, the fear of the outside world now compounded by the internal chaos. My friend texted me to see what I was doing the next day, as he wanted to watch the Toronto Maple Leaf playoff game. I invited him and his family over to watch it here, the safest place I knew. His wife, who is also my friend, is a nurse. I asked her what she thought of the new drugs I had been prescribed, sertraline, also known as Zoloft. She praised how effective they were for many people and strongly encouraged me to try them. I trusted her professional judgment and her genuine care. I finally convinced myself to take the first step the next morning.

So, the next morning arrived. The pills sat on my bedside table, a terrifying promise. As I was about to drive my son to school, I opened the bottle, stared at the small capsule, and with a shaky hand, took one. "Here we go," I said, my voice barely audible, as the new, daunting journey officially began.

I drove my son to school. As I was driving home, sitting at a red light, I felt the anxiety strike. It was an intense, sudden wave where I couldn't catch my breath, and a dizzying sensation made me feel as if I were about to pass out at the wheel. I raced home, barely making it back, and collapsed on the couch. My ears began to ring, a screaming, piercing tinnitus at what felt like a hundred times its normal volume. The sensations of a panic attack were incredibly powerful. I felt as if I weighed 500 pounds and couldn't move. My eyes hurt, unable to focus for more than thirty seconds without a throbbing pain. With my wife at work, I was officially in an attack that was beyond my ability to manage alone. For the first time ever, I reached out for support and called my neighbor, a kind man who had no idea what I was going through. He came over and just talked with me, his calm voice a lifeline, reassuring me that this wasn't a panic attack but likely the drugs entering my system for the first time. I started documenting how I felt, hour by hour, so I could monitor for any improvement. He didn't leave my side until I felt back in control, which seemed to be about four hours later. Once he left, a heavy haze rolled over me, a strange, disconnected feeling. I didn't like it. I felt like a stranger in my own body. I was constantly dizzy, and just going up the stairs to use the washroom required extra caution and slow, deliberate movements.

The next day was the exact same experience, with the same intensity and at the same time, except, as I've said before, the sensations were even stronger. I called my neighbor again. He, of course, sat with me until I felt better. It was clear that taking these drugs in the morning was impairing my ability to function.

I chose to take it in the evening from this point forward.

The first night I took the pill, the experience was profoundly difficult. I was so dizzy, like waking from anesthesia, that talking became a monumental task. Forget standing, forget moving, forget relaxing. I was physically a zombie, but my mental state was even more active, racing and terrified. I was living my worst nightmare, every fear I had of previous anxiety was exactly this: medicated, out of control, and unable to move. I was now officially living in my head, having a panic attack, while my physical body lay there, unable to move or communicate.

I woke up the next morning into a new routine of feeling the effects of the drug wearing off, the heightened anxiety as high as it could be, while trying to eat, drink, and stay physically active. The dizziness and tinnitus remained. Every night, when taking the pill, the same harrowing situation would happen. I asked my wife to stay home from work that week, as I was no longer independent. I needed help to do everything. My mom came to stay with us so my wife could go back to work. During this time, I developed a new fear: agoraphobia. I wasn't able to leave my room without inducing a panic attack. I couldn't even go to the washroom, as the effects were so strong that standing would set off another episode. I accepted my current life as a terrifying new reality. My body, my brain, my mind were all disconnected from each other, and not one part of me knew how to react, causing me, the physical person, to live in a constant state of survival mode. My mom did not leave my side, and I fully leaned on her support, a vulnerability I had never allowed myself.

As I continued with the Zoloft for two more days, I recognized that being awake was too difficult, that the only relief I had was being asleep. I called the pharmacy and explained the situation. They said, "Wow, no, call your doctor and stop right now." I was able to contact my doctor and tell him what was happening. He agreed and told me to stop. He gave me a prescription for a different type of medication, a journey filled with so much disappointment.

18

A Journey into the Void

The prescription for the new medication, venlafaxine, sat on my counter, an unnerving promise of a different path. After the terrible experience with sertraline, I was more than nervous. I was deeply reluctant. I had been living in a constant state of anxiety and panic, a raw, exposed nerve. The medication had pushed me to my absolute limit, unable to even complete the simple tasks of daily life. I had a virtual therapy session that day, and the terror of it all was so overwhelming that I had a panic attack right there on the phone. My therapist, for the first time, was a direct witness to the dark, chaotic hell I had been living in. I knew, without a doubt, that I couldn't continue like this. I had to try something new. Despite my fear, and with my mom and son with me, I swallowed the pill at dinner, a hesitant leap of faith. The thought of feeling like I did before was a heavy burden, but I took it anyway, a regrettable necessity.

I counted it. Twenty-four minutes later, I felt the effects come on. At first, it was a heavy-set headache and a wave of dizziness. Anxiety immediately set in, progressively getting stronger. My mom, sitting with me, talked, her voice a steady presence, asking how I was doing. Every five minutes, the sensations intensified. The tinnitus returned, so strong that I couldn't hear her over the screaming in my ears. Panic officially took over, a force more powerful than it had ever been. I wanted to take a Xanax, but I worried about overdosing or having a negative reaction. I decided it was a good idea to call the pharmacy to ask if this was normal. They said yes, but advised me to inform my doctor. It was eight o'clock at night. I couldn't do that. I took the Xanax anyway. My mom, recognizing my distress, decided it was best to call 911. My body, consumed by the panic, had become so weak that I could barely see my phone or have the strength to use my fingers to call. She took over, speaking with the operator, calmly explaining that I had taken new medication and Xanax and was in crisis.

Once off the phone, my mom called my son down to chat and let him know that 911 had been called and that I might be going to the hospital tonight. I managed to say out loud, "I am not taking these fucking drugs anymore as it's ruining my life." It had been nine consecutive days of mental torture, a relentless siege on my soul.

I know there are many drugs that can help, and I'm fully aware that it takes time for them to work. But for me, the immediate effects were much stronger than what was expected, to the point where, and yes, I will say it, I understand why people commit suicide. The feeling of losing yourself, being trapped in a dark hole with no way out, feeling heavy, out of control, stripped of all joy, love, and any positive emotion, it's gone. I'm not that person to ever do that, but I can definitely empathize with someone in that headspace. It is one hundred percent real. I'll elaborate on this shortly.

Once the paramedics arrived, I managed to get my heart rate and breathing under control. I expressed my worry about overdosing and explained that it's better to be safe than sorry when it comes to situations like this. They were very empathetic and assured me that I had made the right call. I was still unable to move and extremely dizzy, but the panic began to dissipate as the Xanax kicked in. They informed me that I could go to the hospital, but because my heart rate and blood pressure were as good as someone just relaxing, the hospital probably couldn't do anything for me other than monitor me. I decided against it, knowing I'd rather be at home with my mom, like old times, than sit in a hospital to wait it out. They assured me I could call back anytime if things progressed and it wouldn't be a hindrance to them. I thanked them kindly.

I sat on the couch, now worried about my son and wondering what was going on in his mind as he had to watch me fall apart. I managed to get to his bedroom, laid down with him, and had a father-son talk about what I was going through. I reassured him I wasn't going to die, but that I was going through my own personal hell, and that unfortunately, he had to see it. He expressed his worry for me and said he didn't want to lose me and missed doing fun things with me. We both cried, and I promised him I would get better no matter what. He then fell asleep in a better state of mind, knowing there was something to look forward to.

I told my mom I wanted to go to sleep. My wife arrived home, and both of them helped me to bed. Dizzy, exhausted, broken, and defeated, I closed my eyes and waited for a new day—a new day I promised myself I wouldn't be taking any more of these meds.

I woke up at 6 a.m. feeling okay. There were no anxious thoughts like before. I enjoyed the peace I had craved for so long. Around 7 a.m. I stood up. The dizziness returned, and as I walked to the washroom, a sensation all too familiar rushed over me: an intense, metallic fuzz rushing through my body, just as I had felt as a kid going into surgery.

Instantly, I reverted to my childlike state of fear, dread, and terror. It claimed my very soul. And I knew at this moment, with a chilling certainty, this was it. The moment I had been waiting for, the moment I had worked hard to get to, my official new mental rock bottom. I rushed back to my bed, my body, my brain, my mind all collapsed, completely overwhelmed. My wife came to check on me, and I managed to say, "I'm not well." Full-blown, uncomfortable, uncontrollable panic set in.

She helped calm me down by distracting me, having me count backward from sixty to zero, with the intention of bringing the panic down. It was working. I was able to manage it. Then, it came back, this time more powerful, stronger than when I called 911. I could feel something building, a volcano about to explode. She helped me again, counting from sixty down to zero, and it subsided again. At this time, I mentioned, "Maybe we look at going to a mental hospital because this is out of control." And then it came back a third time. This time, even stronger. I couldn't breathe. My brain now assumed I was going to die. This is it. This is how I'm going to die. At least I had my wife and mom with me.

The climax of the panic attack had been building in a way that felt utterly apocalyptic. My wife was trying to ground me, to bring me back from the brink, but a third, even more powerful wave of terror rolled over me. I couldn't breathe. My brain, now convinced of my impending death, had accepted it as a certainty. There was nothing left to fight for, no more energy to push back against the inevitable.

And then, just as the volcano was about to explode, something spectacular and involuntary happened. I felt a sudden, visceral surge to let go. It wasn't a conscious decision to stop fighting; it was a physical and psychological surrender. The panic, the fear, the resistance—it all just stopped. And in that instantaneous surrender, the eruption happened.

It was an outpouring of emotion and energy unlike anything I have ever experienced.

An all-encompassing **euphoria**, as if a dam that had held back a lifetime of pressure had finally broken. It rushed over me, a feeling of ascending, of being lifted out of my body and into a state of pure, weightless peace.

I started to cry hysterically, but these weren't tears of fear or pain anymore; they were tears of release. I could physically feel the anxieties and panic, which had felt like heavy, suffocating presences, being expelled from me. It was like they were being choked out, punched in the face, a tangible force being annihilated. All the negativity, all the accumulated torment, was being purged from my very soul. A sense of soul, a higher energy, filled the space left behind.

As that incredible surge of euphoria started to fade, it didn't leave a void. It left a perfect **silence**. My mind, which had been a constant battlefield of racing thoughts and screaming fears, was suddenly quiet. Still. Empty. Peaceful. Calm. It was as if a tornado had ravaged a community, destroying everything in its path, but now the sun was shining, and people were slowly emerging from their protective holes, looking around at the ruins, no longer afraid.

I had finally hit my rock bottom. The terror, the anxiety, the stress, the darkness, the torment. I recognized with an unshakeable certainty that it could not get any worse than what I had just experienced. And in that recognition, there was a newfound peace. My fear was gone. My anxiety was gone. I could sit quietly, with a quiet mind, and for the first time in my life, I felt as if I was truly and finally on the road to recovery.

The battle was over, and the long, difficult work of rebuilding could begin. The morning after the panic volcano erupted, I woke up to a world that felt both familiar and utterly alien. For the first time in my life, a peaceful silence had replaced the constant, humming anxiety in my mind. The air in my bedroom felt lighter, the light from the window seemed gentler. I felt a sense of relief and peace so pure, it was almost overwhelming. The chaos of the past nine days—the constant attacks, the terror, the feeling of losing myself—had finally subsided, leaving behind an unshakeable stillness. But in this stillness, I noticed a new, quieter kind of fear. I was still scared of things: driving, going out in public, talking with people who were not in my immediate social circle.

The impossible walk had reimagined itself as a new battle I had to wage. I knew the name for it now: agoraphobia. I understood why it had happened—my brain, in its effort to protect me, had designated the outside world as unsafe—but the task of overcoming it was equally, if not more, difficult than battling the panic itself. The road to recovery was not a highway; it was an unplanned city centre under construction, riddled with detours, and gridlock. Every step was tiny, deliberate and terrifying. Each day, I had to push and force myself to get more comfortable doing things. The process started small: I would stand at my bedroom door, then make myself walk down the hallway to the living room. The next day, I would make it a point to stand at the front door, just opening it a crack to feel the outside air. Then, the ultimate challenge: walking down the driveway. Every step was a conscious effort to fight the rising tide of anxiety. My daily goal was simple: do more than yesterday, so I could eventually get back to work and live my life as normal, without anxiousness interrupting my daily tasks.

I upped my therapy sessions to one or two times a week, as I was finally seeing a tangible benefit in talking, in verbalizing the very things I had suppressed for so long. Every day became a new turning point, marked by a small, personal victory—another thing I was able to do without the fear of anxiety looming over me. *My* determination, *my* perseverance, and *my* deep-seated want to get better had become my sole driving force. I was an active participant in my own healing, not a passive victim waiting for the next attack.

Yes, anxiety will be a part of my life forever, I know this now. But with help, with a supporting team of friends and family, I truly believe I can battle this demon that has tried to control me for so long. My road to recovery is not complete, but it is good enough to tell a story. I will continue to seek therapy, and I will continue to be open and tell my story for anyone who wants to hear it. I am more active rather than reactive.

I also want to share a few things that I've learned on this journey that might help inspire you if you are ever feeling anxious or feel like you cannot cope. For example, listening to music has been incredibly helpful for me. Music is a raw emotion, and listening to specific songs has helped me ground myself and stay present in the moment. It has been scientifically proven that it can lower depression and anxiety.

Another thing is what they call the 90-second rule: most emotions, even the most overwhelming ones, last about 90 seconds unless you keep fueling them with your thoughts. If you're anxious, let the feeling pass without attaching a story to it. Don't tell yourself, "This is it, I'm dying." Just feel the sensation and let it pass. Your brain loves to prove itself right, so whatever you expect, your mind will find evidence for. Tell yourself, "This will be fun," before a social event, and your brain will actively filter for things that make that true. This works because of selective attention bias; you literally start seeing what you believe. The hard part is letting that belief be true. With practice, you can and you will be able to do that thing you want to do.

Most people are living life on autopilot, doing the same thing, day in and day out. But the same habits lead to the same results. They are either building their future or repeating their past. Make that decision intentionally, to change for the better.

I also wanted to mention that we fear hitting rock bottom like it's the end. But I've found that it often forces us to create real change in our lives. The real enemy is the comfortable middle—where things aren't bad enough to change, but aren't good enough to thrive. My goal with therapy was intentionally getting to this point, to find my rock bottom, so I could start to heal. You need to structure this properly because it can get very dark and could be dangerous. So, seek guidance, create your support group full of trustworthy family or friends. You should not do it alone.

If you ever feel like you cannot continue, always reach out to your local authorities, paramedics, or online support groups. There is a way to get the support and help you get through this safely, I promise you this. You just have to do the work yourself.

I'm not a counselor or a therapist. I'm just someone with my own lived experiences, telling my story in hopes that it can help someone see a different perspective on things. Everyone's anxiety is different and difficult, but we can all get through it together. Get yourself talking. Tell your story. You'll thank yourself in the end.

Acknowledgments and Gratitude

I want to take some time to pay my respects. My gratitude is not just a polite gesture; it is the foundation of my healing.

To the nurses,

I cannot thank each and every one of you, past and present, for the intense work and care you do day in and day out. You do not get enough credit for the work you do. I remember your gentle smiles after a surgery, your quiet reassurance. Your care, empathy, knowledge, and compassion truly make a difference in moments of utter fear and vulnerability.

To the doctors,

Thank you for literally keeping me alive and giving me the best medical support you could. The knowledge you provide saves people daily. You gave me a chance at a normal life, a chance to grow up and find my way.

To my mother,

You are the rock, the glue that held me together. I couldn't have survived those years without you. I remember your face after every surgery, your quiet determination. I couldn't imagine my life without you by my side through good times and bad. We were meant to be together in this lifetime for a reason.

To my dad,

Thanks for being my hero. Someone I looked up to be like growing up. I'll always cherish our talks and the time we spent together. Your patience and humility taught me a lot about myself and how to be a good man.

To my brother,
Thanks for being a normal older brother to me. Beating me up, playing hockey, and doing all the brotherly things like me being super annoying to you. These were the things I looked forward to the most in my recovery, as this meant normal to me.

To my wife,
Thanks for choosing me, for seeing the good, the bad, the ugly, and the amazing. Thanks for never leaving my side and staying strong even when I was at my weakest. Your unwavering support gave me a safe space to fall apart and then to rebuild. You keep me in line and grounded. We balance each other out.

To my son,

Thank you for teaching me how to be a man. For being my best friend. Watching you grow is a gift that inspires me to be a better man every day.

Love to you all.

Manufactured by Amazon.ca
Bolton, ON

51517911R00097